ISBN: 978-0-615-49870-6

## Thanks to

I want to thank God for putting me in a situation where I had to come up with Islamic arts and crafts ideas to allow children to enjoy Islamic Studies.

Also, I want to thank my parents for teaching me the importance of Islam, my husband for giving me the opportunity to write this book, and my sister Samar for her generosity.

Additionally, I have to thank my children Hadeer, Siraj, and Janna. Because of them I was put in a situation where I had to come up with Islamic projects that are fun and creative.

I would also like to thank my nephews, Zakarea and Dean, who participated in the projects as well.

And last but not least I would like to thank the children at New Horizon Elementary School, Los Angeles who I worked with for three years and was able to test my ideas on.

An additional thanks to Lynn Houri, Henda Kinat Ibrahim, Amal Dahir, Jomana Siddiqui, and all the children who participated in making the projects and/or displays.

Again I thank God and ask Him to reward my family for our intention and may God bless us all.

All proceeds will go to an Islamic educational institution.

*Sahar Sabry Abdel-Aziz*

# Preface

In 1998 when Christmas, Hanukkah, and Ramadan were all celebrated during the month of December, I took my three children, 9-year-old Hadeer, 8-year-old Siraj, and 6-year-old Janna, to Story Time at the local library. With great excitement, the librarian told the wide-eyed children that she would read stories about the holidays in December to them: Christmas and Hanukkah. My daughter Hadeer, almost automatically, said to me, "How about Ramadan, Mommy? That's in December too." After Story Time was over I asked the librarian to share with the children a story about Ramadan too because all three holidays coincided this year. The librarian retorted, "Ramadan is not a fun month; it's a religious holiday."

I proceeded to tell her that like Christmas and Hanukkah, Ramadan is also a religious time and that it is, in fact, fun, just like those two holidays. After a long discussion on this matter the librarian agreed. If I could bring her a children's story about Ramadan she would share it during Story Time at the library. Naturally, I looked in the library for a children's short story about Ramadan. However, to my children's disappointment, and mine, there were none.

That is when I began working with my children on building off of their own experiences to write a story about Ramadan. I also designed an art project for the children to participate in during Story Time the following week at the library. Elhamdulilah, the following week we were ready with a story to share with the children and we made a lantern as the library's art project for the week.

The following year, when I started teaching and developing the Islamic Studies curriculum at New Horizon School in Los Angeles, CA, I asked my students to write short stories about Ramadan. I also requested that they write poems about the Quran, Ramadan, Eid, the Prophet Mohammad (pbuh), and thankfulness. I then worked on developing creative ideas for art projects to bring to life Islamic ideas and help us celebrate Islamic holidays.

Not only did we adapt existing arts and crafts projects already out there to relate them to Islam, we also created brand new ideas and taught the students to relate everything we used to the One who created the materials: God. We taught them that all man-made items are from God's natural creations, such as wax. We asked the students what wax is made of and encouraged them do their research, and come back to class with an answer. "Wax is made from natural things like cattle fat, sugars, and honey," they wrote. Then we asked them what people use wax for. "People use wax for things like crayons, candles, and cosmetics," they'd answer. We wanted to clarify to the students that using their creativity and God's creation, you could produce beautiful art!

I hope my story will encourage other parents to work with their local communities and inspire their children to be proud of and to use their resources to develop their Muslim American identities.

*Sahar Sabry Abdel-Aziz*

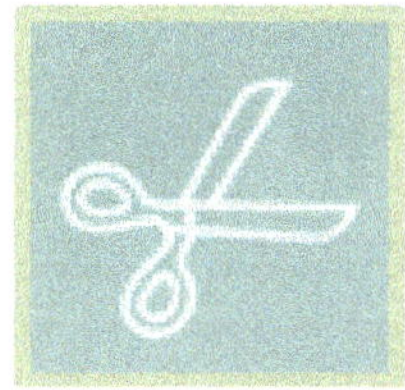

# Table of Contents



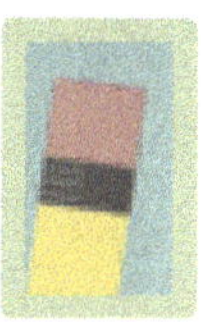

# 3D Kaaba Poster 1

**About:**

Create this picturesque piece of art to hang in your house.

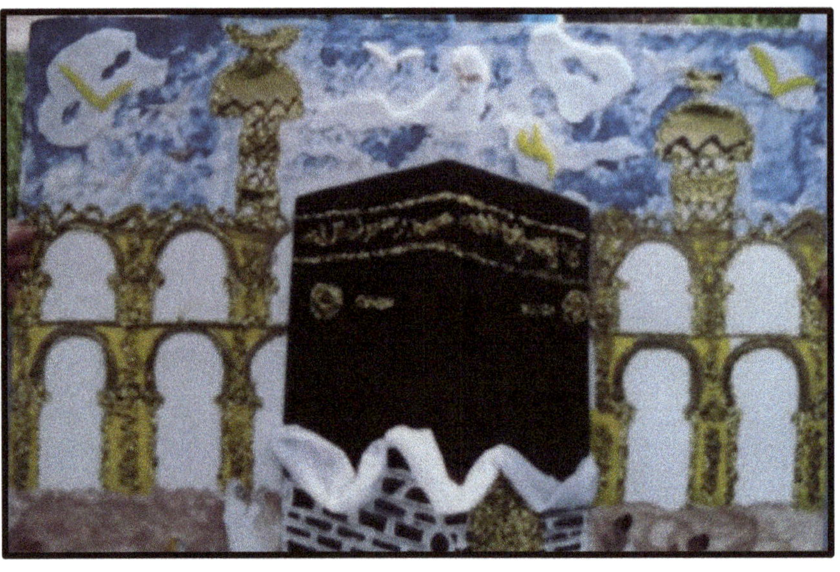

**You will need:**

1 White poster paper

2 Blue paint

3 Pencil

4 Markers

5 Glue

6 Black and brown felt

7 Cotton

8 Gold and silver glitter pens

9 White thin, soft material

10 Scissors

11 Paintbrush

12 Wite-out pen

**What to do:**

1 Draw the Kaaba and the sky on the poster paper.

2 Paint the sky blue and glue cotton in the sky as clouds.

3 Cut the black felt to fit on top of ¾ of the Kaaba.

4 Cut the brown piece of felt and glue it to the remaining ¼ at the bottom of the Kaaba to represent the stones of the Kaaba.

5 Use the wite-out pen to outline the bricks on the brown felt.

6 Cut the white material and glue it on the bottom edge of the black felt in a way that will make the Kaaba cover look rolled up.

7 Use the glitter pens to write an Ayah or two on top of the black area of the Kaaba and you could use them to draw the door of the Kaaba.

8 Use the silver pen to draw the black stone on the side of the Kaaba.

9 Continue decorating the rest of the poster as you please.

# 3D Islamic Art 2

## About:

These 3D art frames make a unique and beautiful piece of artwork.

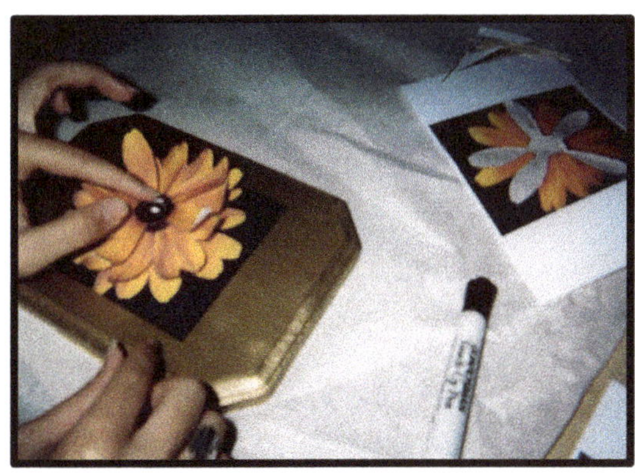

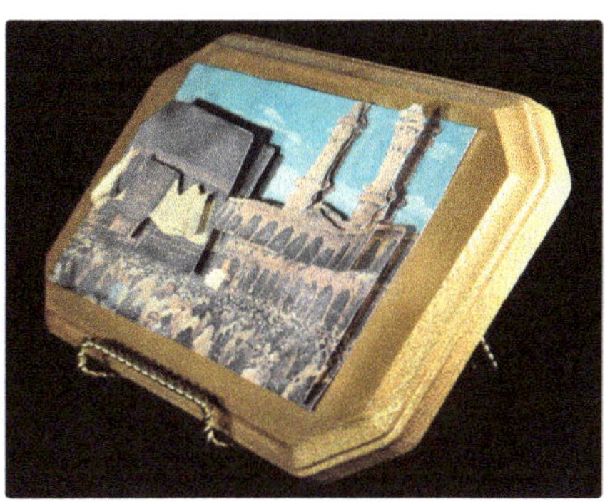

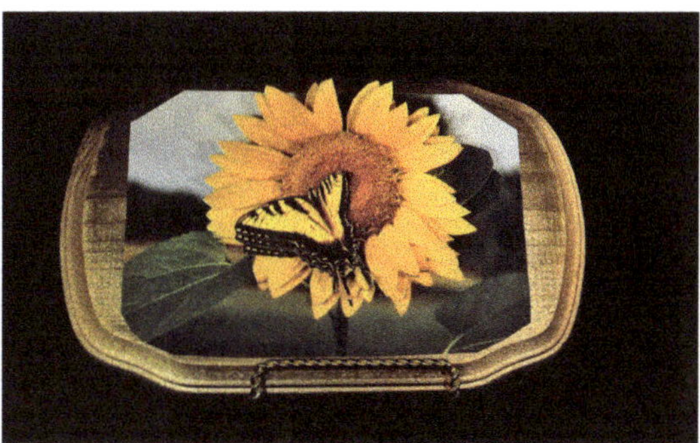

## You will need:

1 5x7-inch piece of decorative wood

2 Three copies of a postcard or picture, photograph, drawing, etc.

3 Large paintbrush

4 Delta Ceramcoat Gleams Acrylic Paint

5 3M Photo Mount Spray Adhesive

6 Polyseamseal Clear Tub & Tile Adhesive Caulk

7 Markers

8 Ultra Clear Protective Acrylic Finish Gloss

9 Scissors

## What to do:

1 Paint the wood using the Delta Ceramcoat Gleams Acrylic Paint.

2 Using the 3M Photo Mount Spray Adhesive, paste the first postcard in the center of the wood.

3 Cut the second postcard to make one part of it stick out.

4 Squeeze the Polyseamseal Clear Tub & Tile Adhesive Caulk onto the first postcard in the parts that you cut in the second postcard.

5 Cut the third postcard to make another part of it stick out.

6 Repeat step 4 for the third postcard.

7 Spray the Ultra Clear Protective Acrylic Finish Gloss on the whole frame.

# Candle Holder Stickers 3

**About:**

These stickers are great for decorating any candle holder. Use them for any occasion such as Eid El Fitr, Eid El Adha, or Hijra.

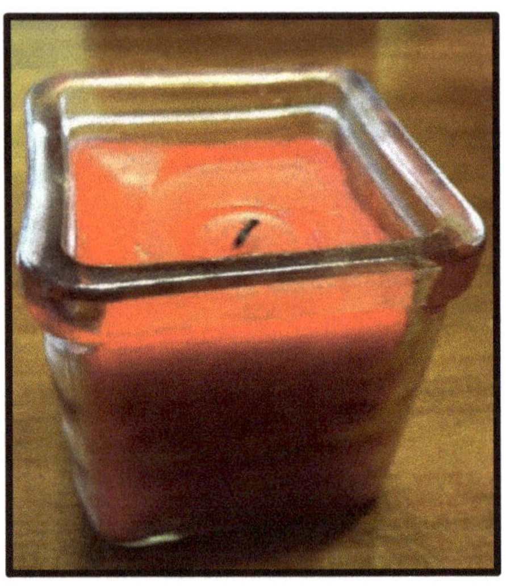

**You will need:**

1 Stickers
(Order: www.simplyimpressions.com)

2 Glass candle holder

3 Candle or wax to make

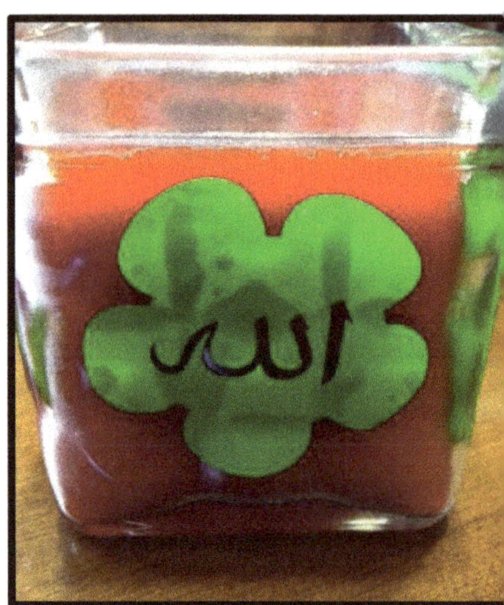


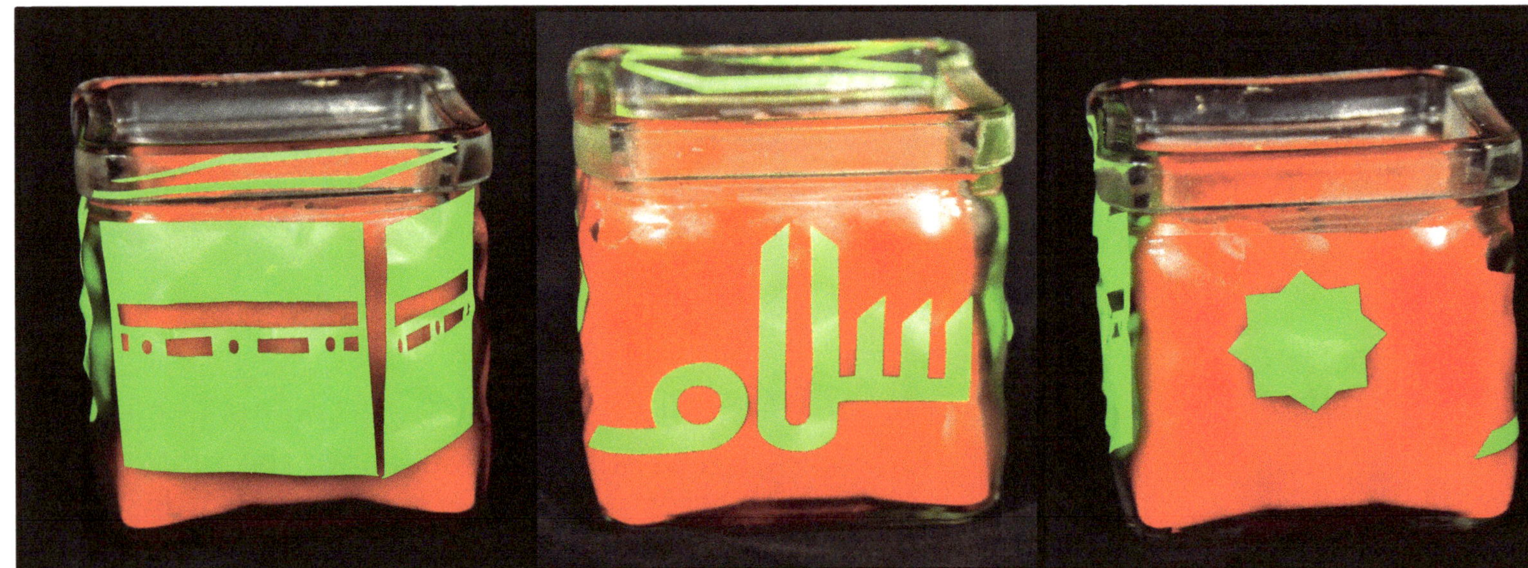


**What to do:**

1 Place stickers you desire around the glass candle holder.

2 Put the ready-made candle in the glass candle holder.

3 Or make your own candle using the wax and pour it in the holder.

# Candles in Pottery
# 4

## About:

Try this creative and different way to make candles with just a few simple steps. Decorate your pot with Islamic writing and give them to your loved ones as gifts to light up their rooms.

## You will need:

1 Clay pottery

2 Wax

3 Wick

4 Paint and paintbrush

5 Shells

6 Sand

7 Pot

8 Stove

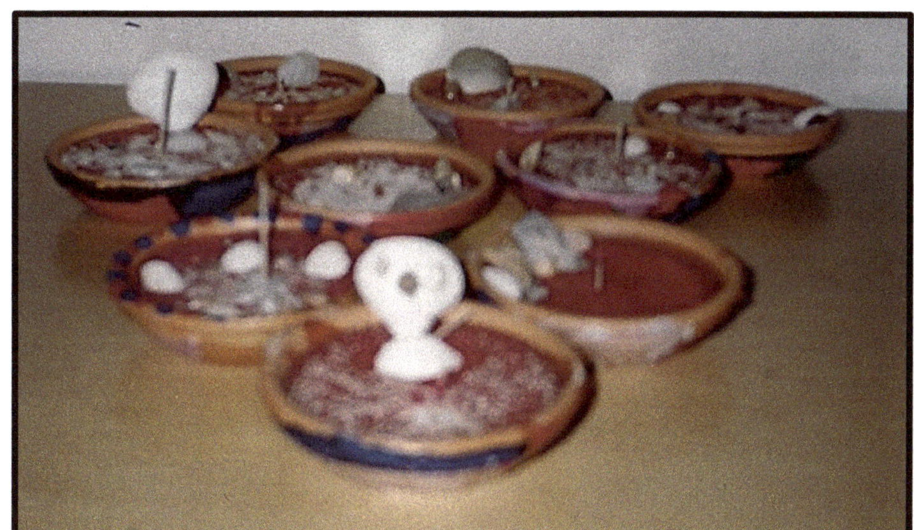

## What to do:

1 Paint the outside of the pottery any way you want.

2 Put the wax in a pot and melt it on stove.

3 Pour the wax into the pottery.

4 Before it dries, place the wick in the center, place shells in the wax, and sprinkle some sand on top for decoration.

5 Leave out to dry.

# Ceramic Plates Art
## 5

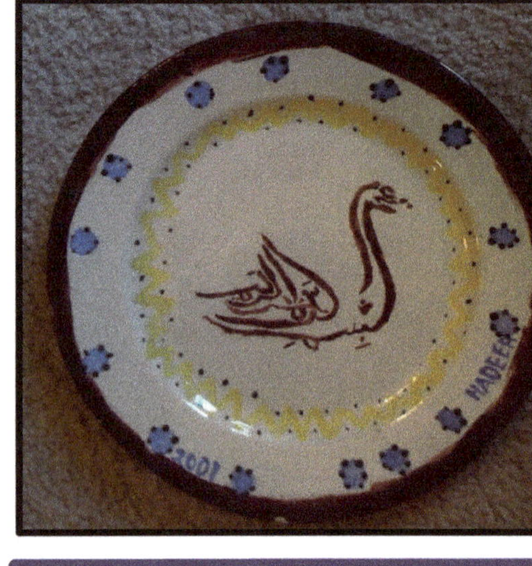


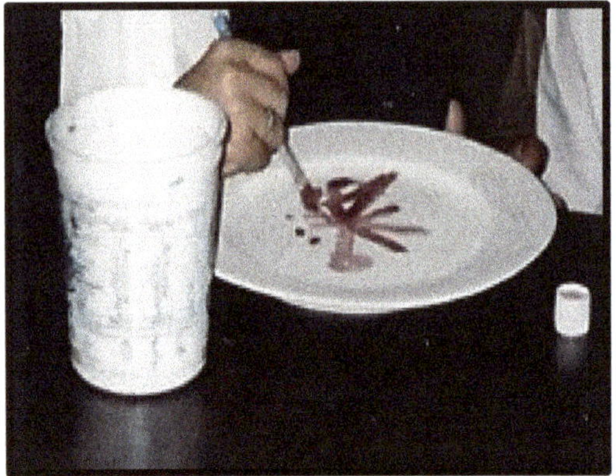

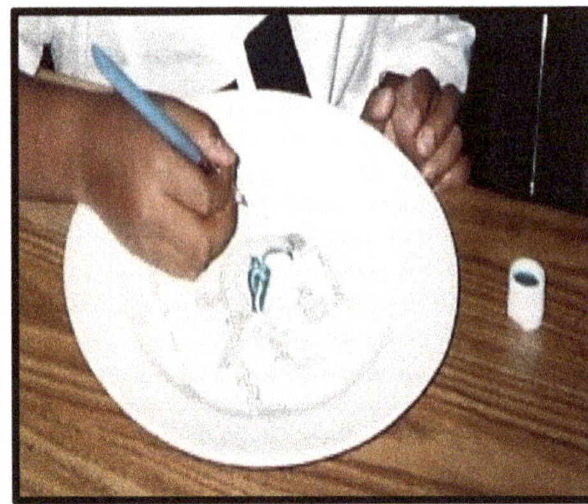

### About:

Take your friends and family to this fun filled store: Color Me Mine.

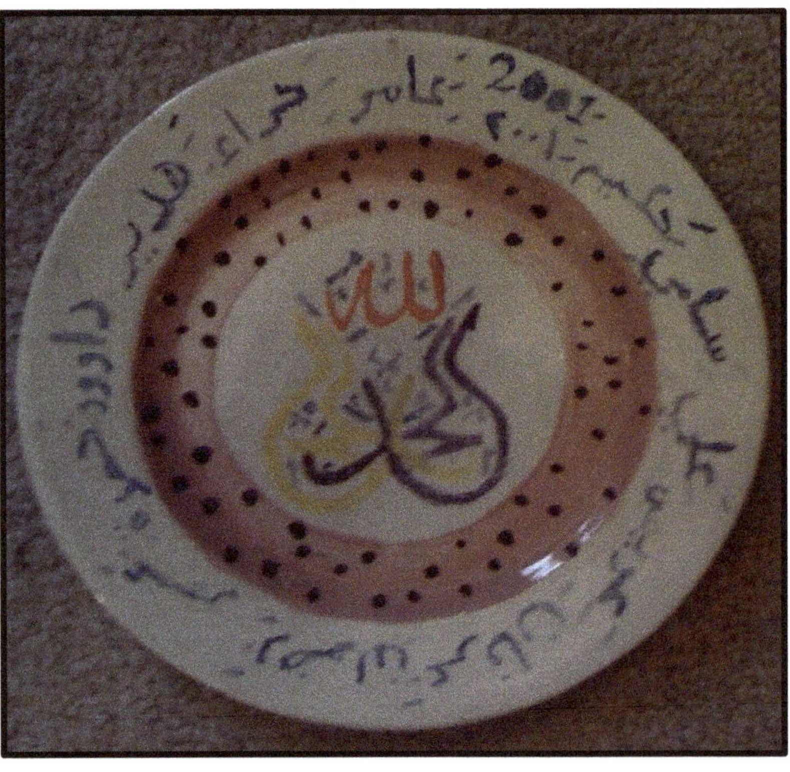

### You will need:

1 Color Me Mine location
(Visit: www.colormemine.com)

2 Plain white ceramic plate

3 Pencil

4 Stencil

5 Paint and paintbrush

6 Clear glaze

7 Kiln

### What to do:

1 Visit a Color Me Mine location near you.

2 Choose your plate.

3 Paint your Islamic Design.

4 The rest is done by store staff.

# Colorful Prayer Carpets
## 6

### About:

Make your own personalized carpet for your daily prayers. Give them as gifts to your friends or family, use them to pray with, or hang them on the wall for decoration. Making these will teach your kids precision cutting, Arabic writing, and safety

### You will need:

1 8x11 piece of fabric material

2 Colored yarn

3 Scissors

4 Colored construction paper

5 Ruler

6 Glue

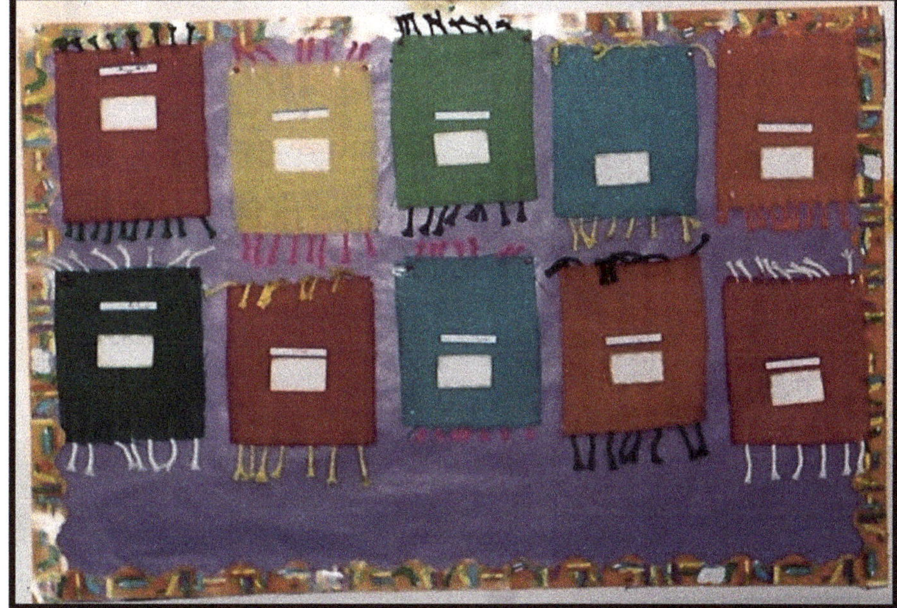

### What to do:

1 Cut a piece of 8x11-inch fabric.

2 Cut yarn into 20 one-inch pieces.

3 Glue 10 yarn pieces on each eight-inch edge of the fabric.

4 On a small piece of construction paper write a small chapter or verse from the Quran.

# Crystal Designs
# 7

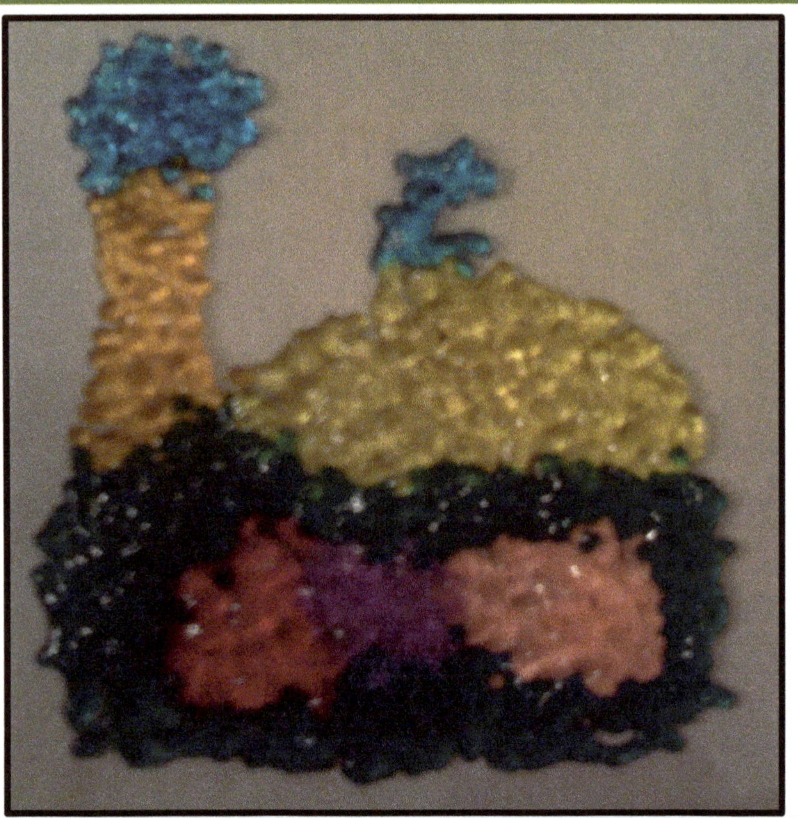

## About:

Ever played with a Makit & Bakeit set? Try this very similar project with Islamic figures like mosques, crescents, Qurans, etc. There are endless combinations of shapes and colors to be creative with.

## You will need:

1 Plastic baking crystals

2 Heavy-duty cookie sheet

3 Foil

4 Tweezers

5 Oven

6 Pencil

7 Spoon

## What to do:

1 Pre-heat oven to 375 degrees.

2 Cover cookie sheet with foil.

3 With a pencil trace the shape you want, like a mosque, into the foil.

4 Choose the colors you want for your shape and spoon the crystals 1/8-inch thick within the shape outline drawn on the foil. Start by placing the crystals in the center of the shape.

5 Make sure there are no large gaps between colors.

6 Use tweezers to move any crystals that fall in the wrong areas.

7 Use the back of the spoon to even out the edges of the shape.

8 Place cookie sheet into the oven and bake for five to ten minutes until crystals have melted and fused together, then leave to cool outside.

# Decorate Arabic Writing
## 8

**About:**

Decorate your house for Eid or Ramadan with this colorful and creative project. Use them for wall art or give them as gifts.

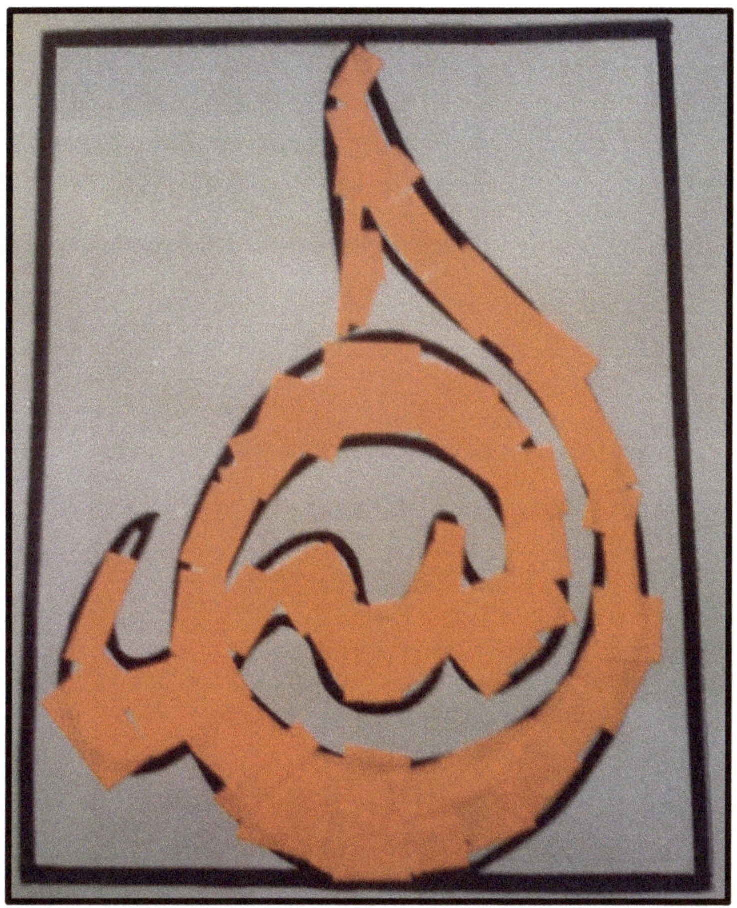

**You will need:**

1 White construction paper

2 Black marker

3 Decorative materials:

- Glitter, glue, paint, tissue paper...

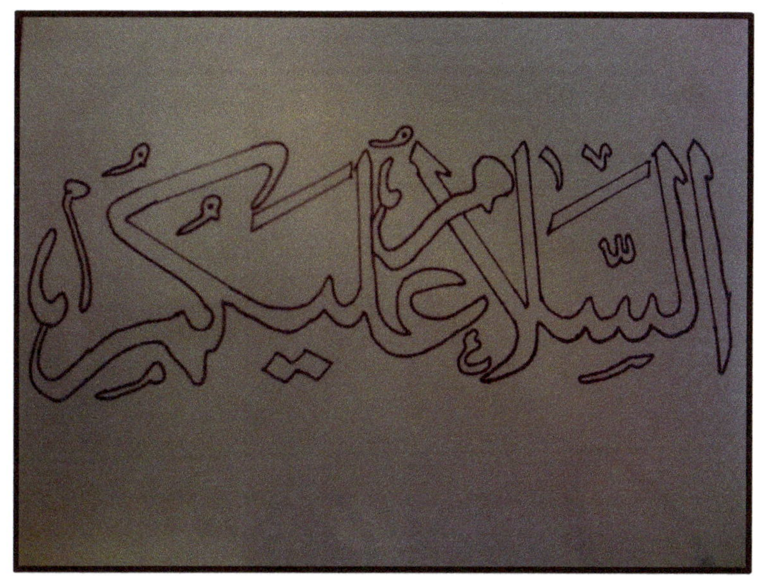


**What to do:**

1 Choose a word, chapter, or sentence from the Quran.

2 Copy it using a black marker on a white piece of construction paper.

3 Make the writing bubble writing like the picture above.

4 Decorate the writing using any decorative materials you like.

5 Hang on a wall framed or unframed.

# Decorate with Date Seeds

# 9

## About:

In Ramadan we eat a lot of dates! Dates are an excellent source of fiber, potassium, and magnesium. But what should you do with the seeds after you've eaten them? Decorate! With the endless possibilities, this project will really show your kid's creativity.

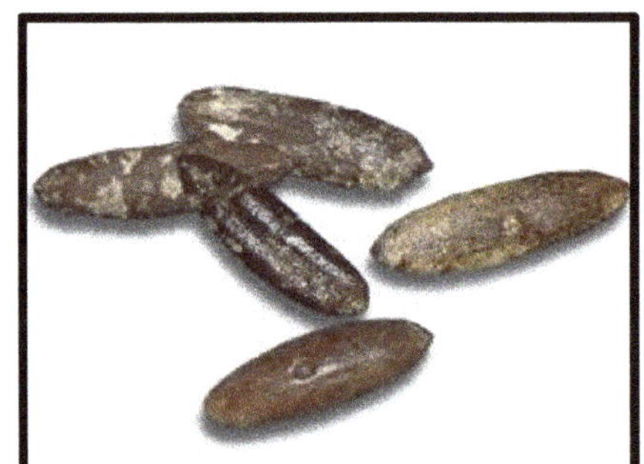

## You will need:

1 Clean date seeds

2 Plain picture frame

3 Decorating materials: paint and paintbrush, string, glitter, dried pasta tissue paper...

## What to do:

1 Wash the date seeds.

2 Paint the picture frame and let it dry.

3 Decorate the frame by gluing the seeds and other materials.

4 Let it dry.

# Decorative Bead Designs

# 10

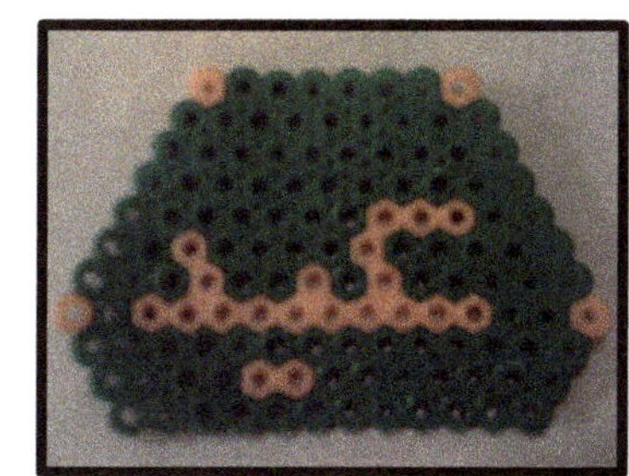

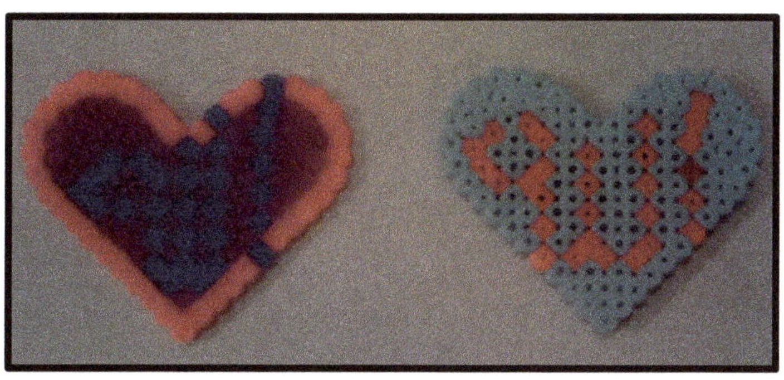

**About:**

Bead designs are fun to make and fun to have. They give children a chance to be creative while practicing counting, planning, and sorting skills. A finished design can be used as decoration, jewelry, bookmarks, key chains, fridge magnets, and gifts for Ramadan, Eid, or anytime of the year.

**You will need:**

1 Fuse beads

2 Peg board

3 Iron

4 Iron board

5 Ironing paper

**What to do:**

1 Working on a flat surface, create your design by placing the beads one by one on the peg board. Follow the pattern and be creative with the design inside the pattern.

2 Preheat a dry household iron to medium setting.

3 Cover the beads with the ironing paper and gently iron the beads in a circular motion for about 30 seconds to fuse the beads evenly.

4 Once the design is cool, peel the paper off and flip the design over.

5 Cover the other side with the paper and iron the other side to fuse it evenly.

# Dried Fruit & Nut Jars
# 11

## You will need:

1 Clear jar with lid

2 Different kinds of dried fruit: peaches, plums, dates...

3 Different kinds of nuts: walnuts, almonds...

4 Two plain sticker labels

5 Wrapping paper

6 Ribbon

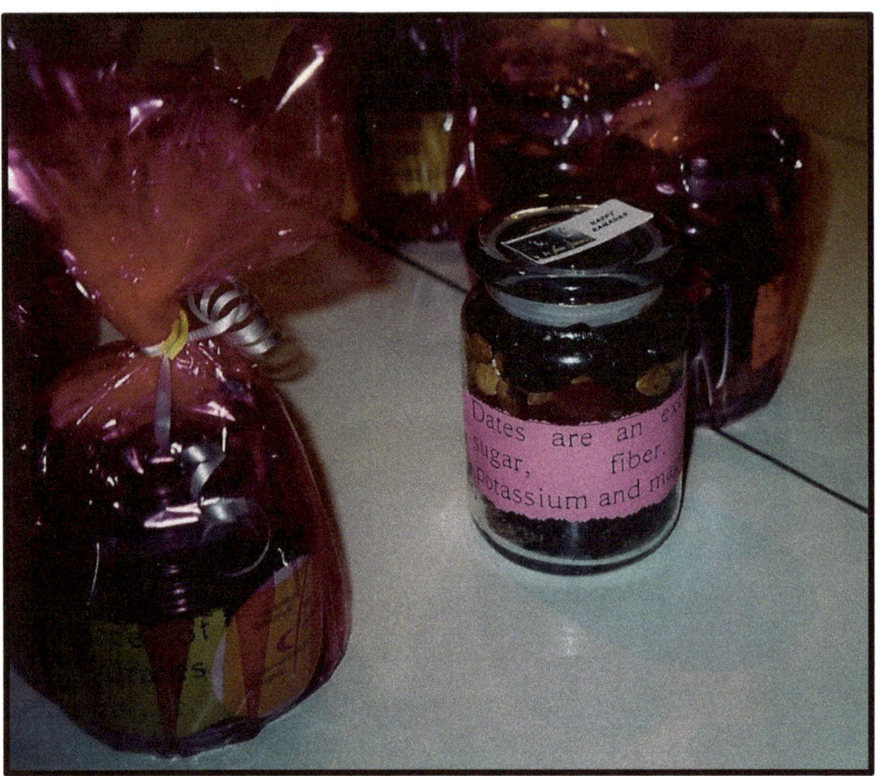


## About:

Try this easy but elegant gift for Ramadan. These dried fruit and nut jars are fun to make, healthy to eat, and make a good gift for any age.

## What to do:

1 Clean the jar and lid.

2 Place dried fruits and nuts in layers or mixed together inside jar.

3 Fill the jar to the top then cover it with the lid.

4 On the sticker label write down the ingredients of the jar and their health benefits.

5 Stick label on jar.

6 Add another sticker to the jar saying who the gift is to and from and write “Happy Ramadan.”

# Duaa & Quran in the Masjid

## 12

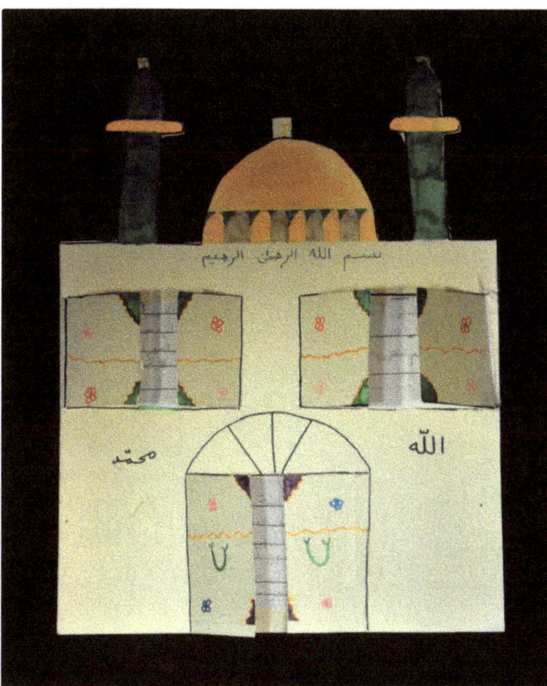

### About:

Use this project to teach your kids the different Duaas (supplications) and/ or Ayahs (verses in the Quran) you use when you enter a Masjid or Ayahs about Ramadan.

### You will need:

1 Manila folder (8.5x11)

2 Pencil

3 Markers

4 Duaa book

5 Quran

6 White paper (8.5x11)

7 Scissors

### What to do:

1 Draw a Masjid with a minaret, dome, windows, and a door on the front of the manila folder.

2 Color the Masjid as you please.

3 Cut the Masjid out as you traced it on the manila folder.

4 Cut the edge of the window from the middle, bottom, and the top.

5 Cut out the edge of the door from the middle, top, and bottom.

6 Write the Duaa you say when you break your fast, the Duaa you say when you enter the Masjid, and/or an Ayah about fasting on white paper.

7 Cut out the Duaas and the Ayah.

8 Open the manila folder and glue the Duaa you say when you enter the Masjid under the opening of the door, glue the Duaa you say when you break your fast under the opening of one of the windows, and glue the Ayah about Ramadan under the opening of the other window.

# Eid Candy Favors
## 13

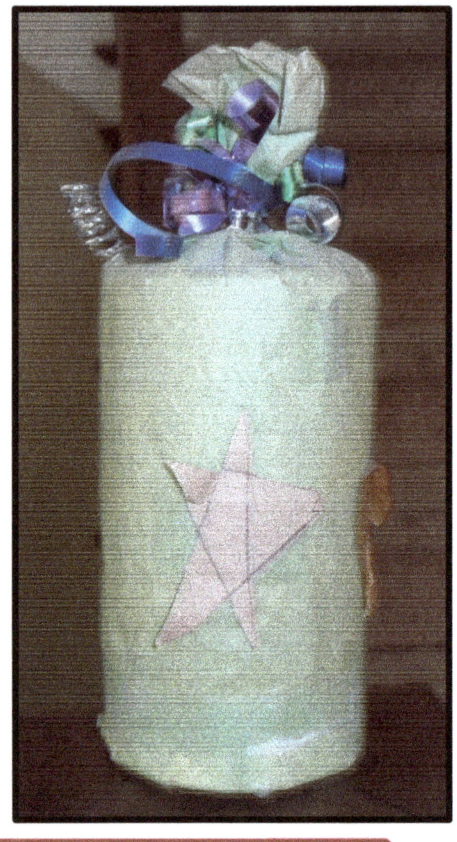

### About:

Put your finished paper rolls to use with this project. This creative way to recycle is fun for Eid or other celebrations. Give them out to your friends as a treat.

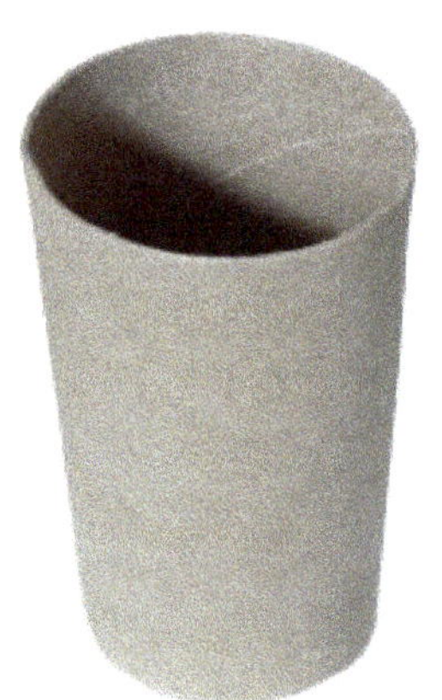

### You will need:

1 Paper roll

2 Colored construction paper

3 Colored tissue paper

4 Scissors

5 Glue

### What to do:

1 Cover the paper roll with glue and put a piece of construction paper to completely cover the roll leaving the two ends open.

2 Cut a 10-inch square of tissue paper and put some pieces of candy in the middle of it.

3 Twist the tissue paper on each end to secure the candy.

4 Insert the tissue paper into the roll.

5 Decorate the outside of the roll.

# Eid Chocolate Roses
## 14

### About:

Want to give someone a rose? What's better than a chocolate filled one that you can unwrap and eat? Make just one or make a whole bouquet and give them to your friends and family on Eid.

### You will need:

1 Two Hershey's Kisses

2 Tape

3 Five-inch square of pink or red plastic wrap

4 Green pipe cleaner

5 Green tissue paper

6 Scissors

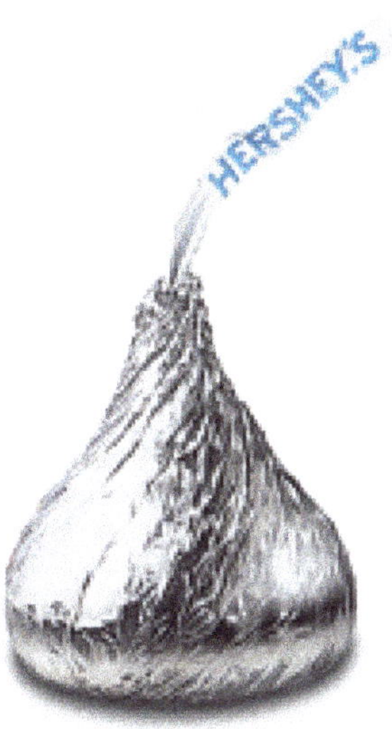


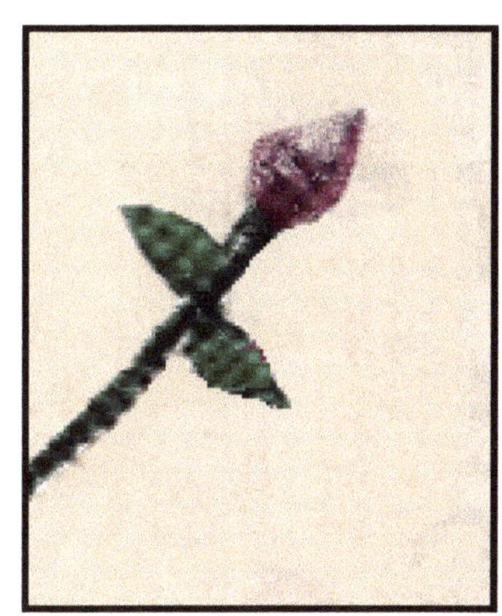

### What to do:

1 For each rose, tape the two chocolates bottom to bottom.

2 Cover them with the plastic wrap making sure there is enough at the bottom to twist into a tail.

3 Tightly twist the top of the pipe cleaner around the tail, creating the stem.

4 Add leaves by holding a long strip of the tissue paper against the stem and rolling the pipe cleaner around the middle of the piece.

5 Cut the leaves to make pointy tips.

6 Wrap tape around the stem part above the leaves to keep it in place.

# Eid Hug Cards
# 15

## You will need:

1 Four sheets of typing paper

2 One sheet of construction paper

3 Markers

4 Crayons

5 Stickers

6 Scissors

7 Glue

8 Tape

## About:

Give the people you love a great big hug this Eid. A hug card that is! This personalized gift will show someone you love how much you care about them.

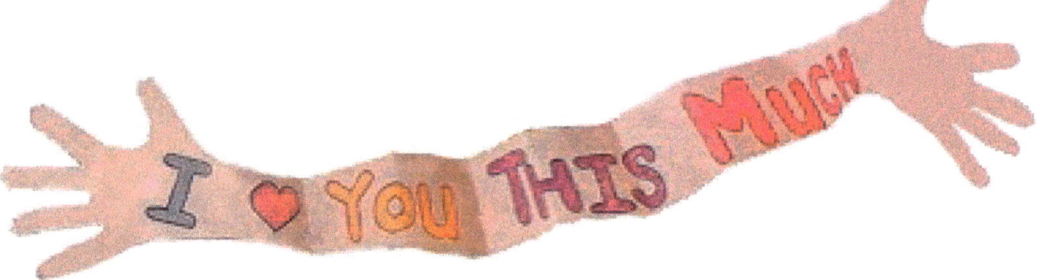


## What to do:

1 Tape the four sheets of paper together end to end.

2 Lay the paper on a hard surface and have someone else trace your arm and hand on half the paper.

3 On the other end trace the other hand and arm and connect them by drawing lines.

4 Use markers, crayons, and stickers to decorate the arms.

5 Write a message across the middle.

6 Fold up the arms till one hand is on top of the other.

7 Fold a piece of construction paper in half like a card and attach the bottom of the right hand inside with glue.

8 Fold the whole thing into the construction paper and write another message on the cover.

# Eid Wreaths
# 16

## About:

Wreaths are great for any holiday. Hang them in your house in indication that Eid is here!

## You will need:

1 Floral wire

2 Flowers

3 Paper

4 Plain wreath

5 Pen

6 Hot glue

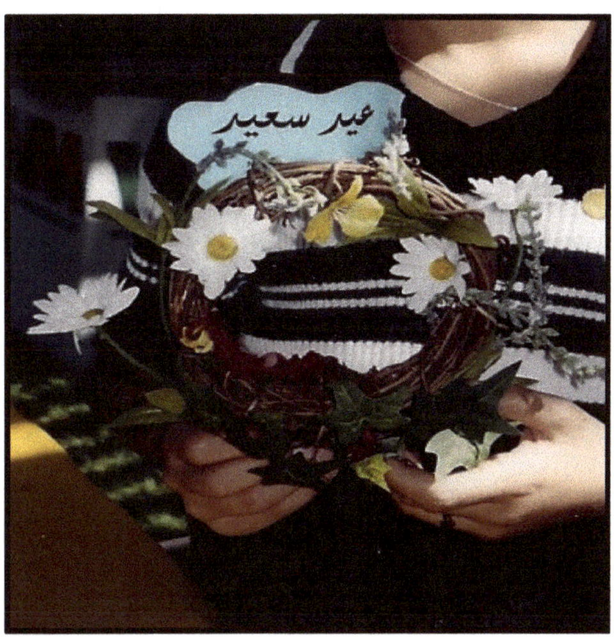


## What to do:

1 Decorate the plain wreath by placing flowers where you want them and wrapping floral wire around them.

2 On a small piece of paper write, in Arabic or English, “Eid Saeed (Happy Eid).”

3 Glue the paper on the wreath anywhere you like.

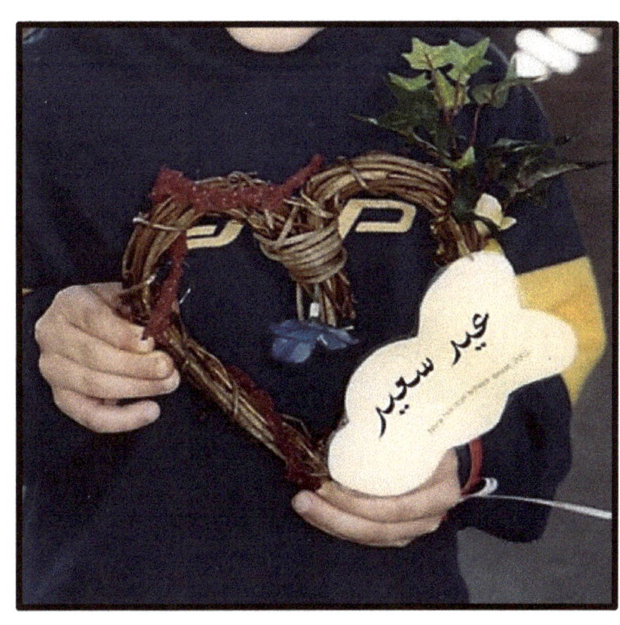

# Gingerbread Mosque
17

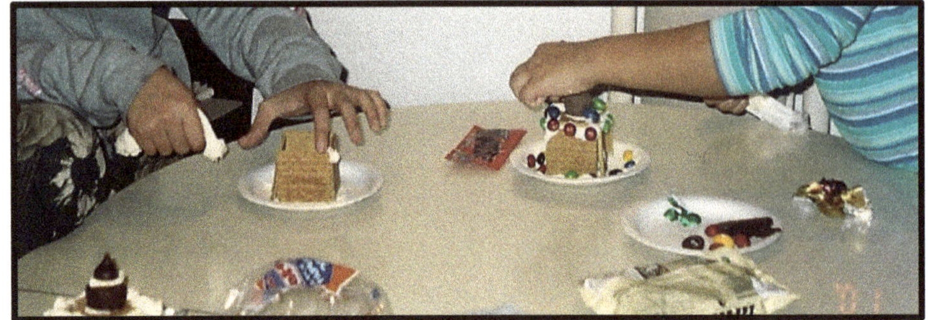

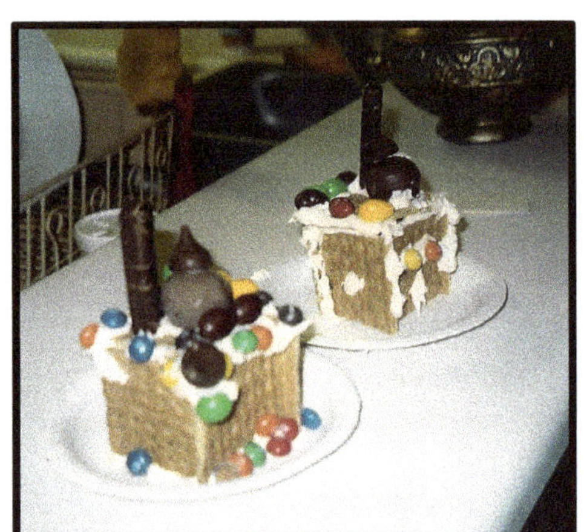

## You will need:

1 Graham crackers

2 Icing

3 M&M candy

4 Hershey's Kisses

5 Kit Kat Bar

6 Any ball-shaped chocolate

7 Paper plate

## About:

You've heard of a gingerbread house, now make a gingerbread mosque... using all the same yummy treats!

## What to do:

1 Place six pieces of square-shaped graham crackers corner to corner to make a cube on the paper plate.

2 Glue all sides together with icing creating the building of the mosque.

3 Decorate the icing with the M&Ms.

4 Place the ball-shaped chocolate on top of the roof in the center to make the dome, using icing as glue.

5 On top of the ball, place one Hershey's Kiss, using icing as glue.

6 Place one stick of Kit Kat on the side of the roof to make a minaret, using icing as glue.

# Hajj Display
## 18

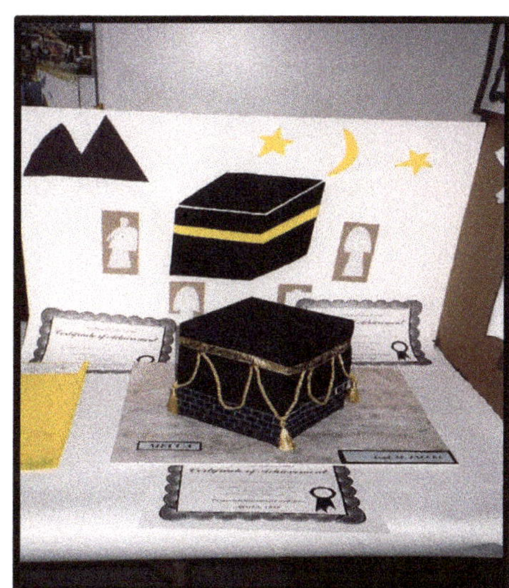

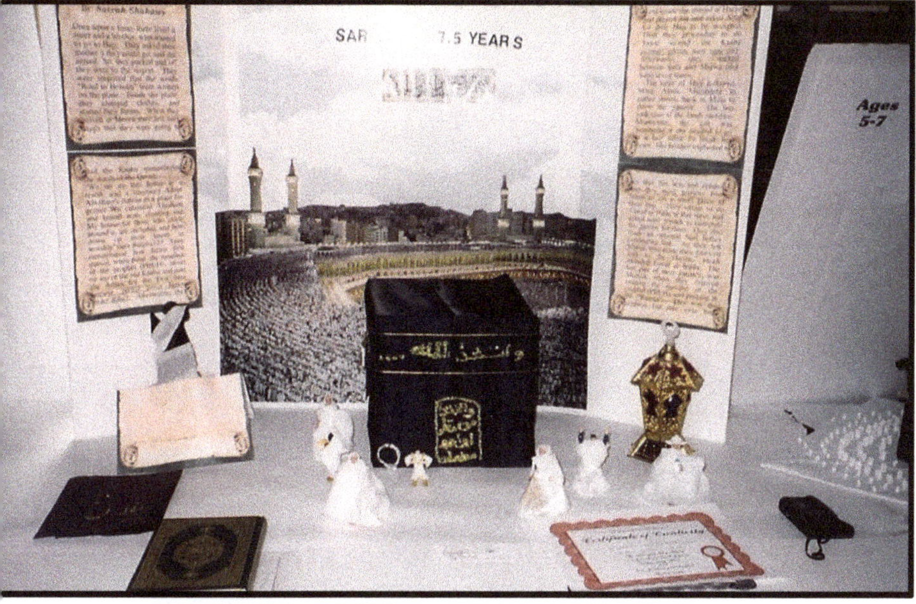

## You will need:

1 Suggested materials:

- Black painted small cube
- Gold string
- Poster board
- Markers, pens, crayons
- Glitter pen
- Globe/map
- Small dolls
- Cotton

2 Glue

## About:

Hajj is an important pillar of Islam. Encourage your children to do their own 3D display about it to present in their classrooms, local library, or to their friends and family to teach others about this pillar.

## What to do:

1 Start with a poster board and write informational sentences about Hajj.

2 Decorate the poster board.

3 On a flat surface, place cube (Kaaba) in the middle and decorate it as well, maybe by following a real life photograph of the Kaaba.

4 Place small dolls around the Kaaba, dress them in white using cotton.

5 Place other related material, like a globe, in the display.

# Happy Holidays Frames
# 19

## You will need:

1 Plain picture frame

2 Small pebbles

3 Paint and paintbrush

4 Glue

5 Small piece of cardboard

6 Toothpick

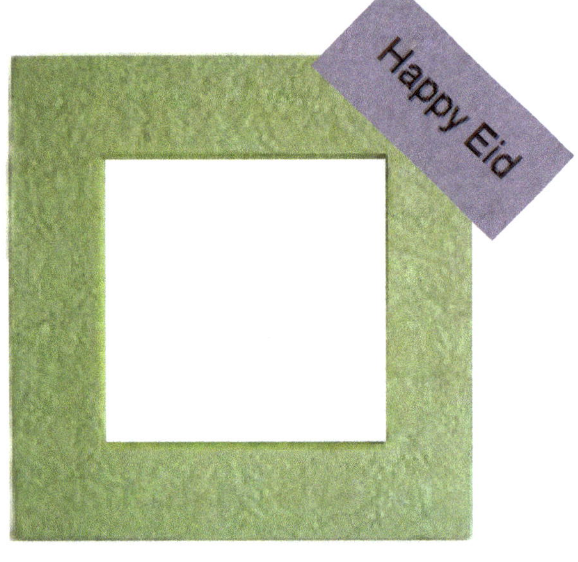


## About:

Another way to decorate and personalize picture frames...Give them as gifts for Ramadan or Eid. This is a chance to really use your creativity.

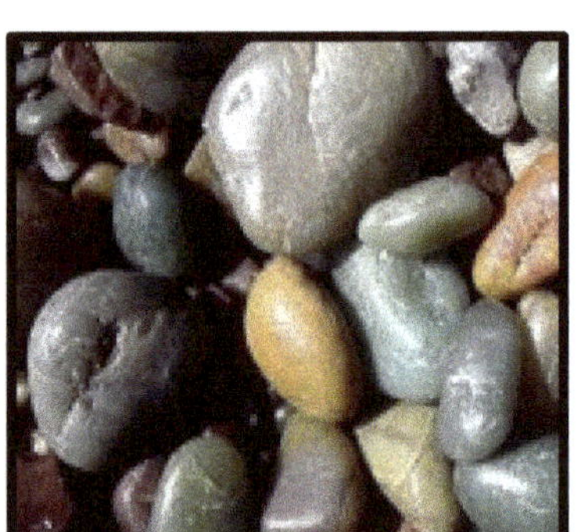

## What to do:

1 Paint the frame any way you want and let it dry.

2 Paint the pebbles and let them dry, or leave them in their natural colors.

3 Paint the piece of cardboard and let it dry.

4 Glue the pebbles onto the frame.

5 Dip the toothpick into the paint and on the cardboard piece, write “Happy Eid” or “Happy Ramadan” and let it dry.

6 Glue the cardboard piece on a corner of the frame.

# Holiday Heart Accordion

# 20

## About:

You can use this accordion this way or in many different ways. You can show the timeline of Prophet Mohamad's life. You could also use this project to show the steps of how a plant grows or how everything in life has a beginning, middle, and an end.

## You will need:

1 Construction paper

2 White paper

3 Markers

4 Glue

5 Scissors

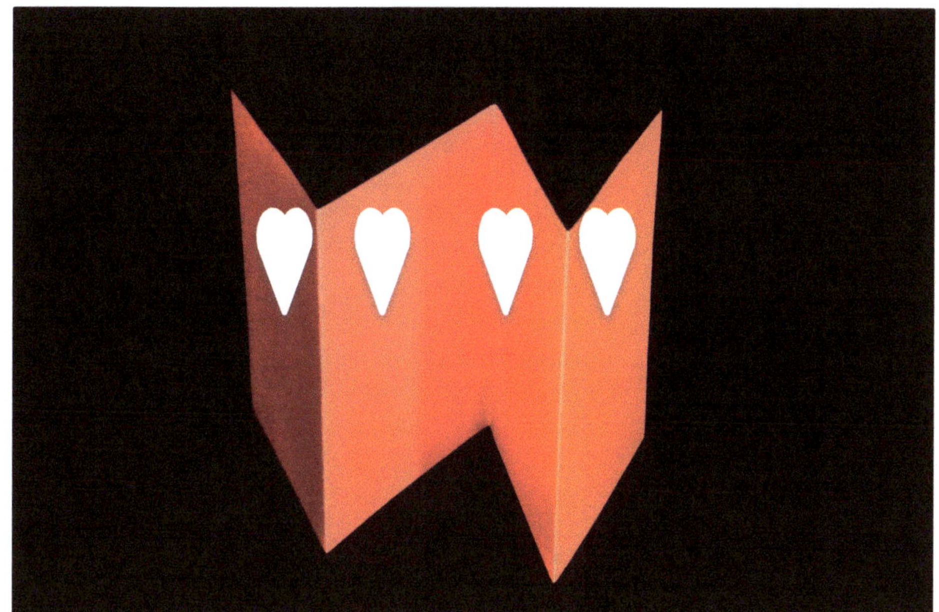

## What to do:

1 Draw 4 hearts on the white paper.

2 Cut out the hearts.

3 Draw or write on each heart why you love Ramadan or Eid.

4 Fold the construction paper into 4 pieces to make it look like an accordion.

5 Glue the hearts on the construction paper.

# Islamic Art Plates
## 21

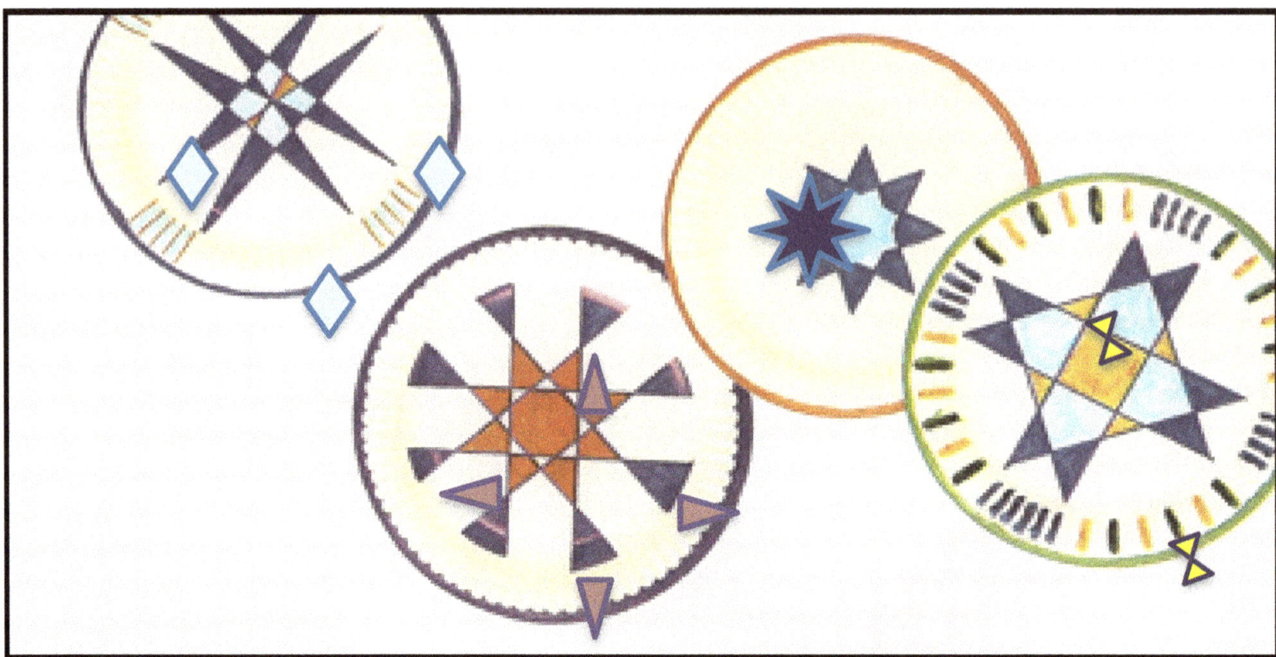

### About:

Islamic art is found everywhere, all over the world on mosques, buildings, paintings, etc. Take this opportunity to make your own, using the same authentic patterns from history. Hang these on your wall as your own artwork.

### You will need:

1 Paper plate

2 Ruler

3 Colored felt-tip pens or paint and paintbrush

4 Pencil

### What to do:

1 With the pencil, make two sets of straight lines across the plate in any direction you want.

2 Join the lines together in any way you want, making a star-like shape.

3 Color in your pattern with several different colors.

# Islamic Mold Designs
## 22

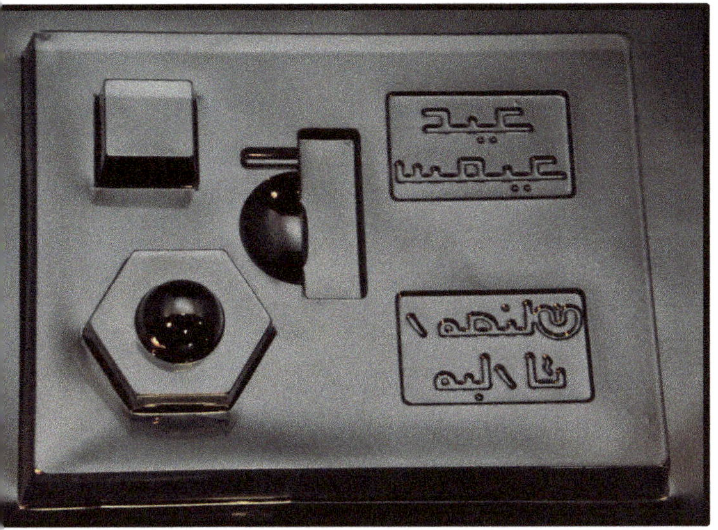

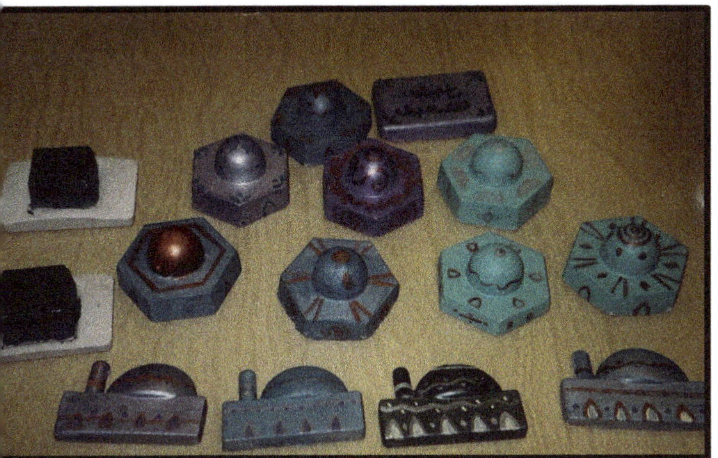

### You will need:

1 Mold with Islamic design
(Order: www.islam4families.com)

2 Plaster, chocolate, soap, or tempera paint

3 Pot

4 Water

5 Paint and paintbrush

6 Stove

### About:

This project is easy, reusable, and inexpensive. All you need is a mold with an Islamic design. These creations make great gifts. You can mold chocolate, plaster, soap, chalk, and much more.

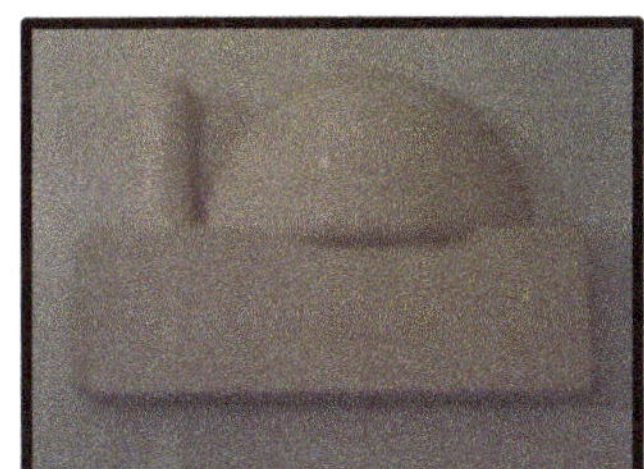

### What to do:

For plaster: 1 Mix plaster with some water. 2 Pour into mold and smoothen out. 3 Wait for it to dry. 4 Paint creation.

For chocolate: 1 Melt chocolate chunks in a pot on stove. 2 Pour into mold. 3 Refrigerate.

For soap: 1 Melt soap cubes in a pot. 2 Pour into mold. 3 Wait for it to cool off and dry.

For chalk: 1 Mix plaster with some water. 2 Mix two tablespoons of tempera paint. 3 Pour into mold. 4 Wait for it to dry.

# Islamic Snow Globes
## 23

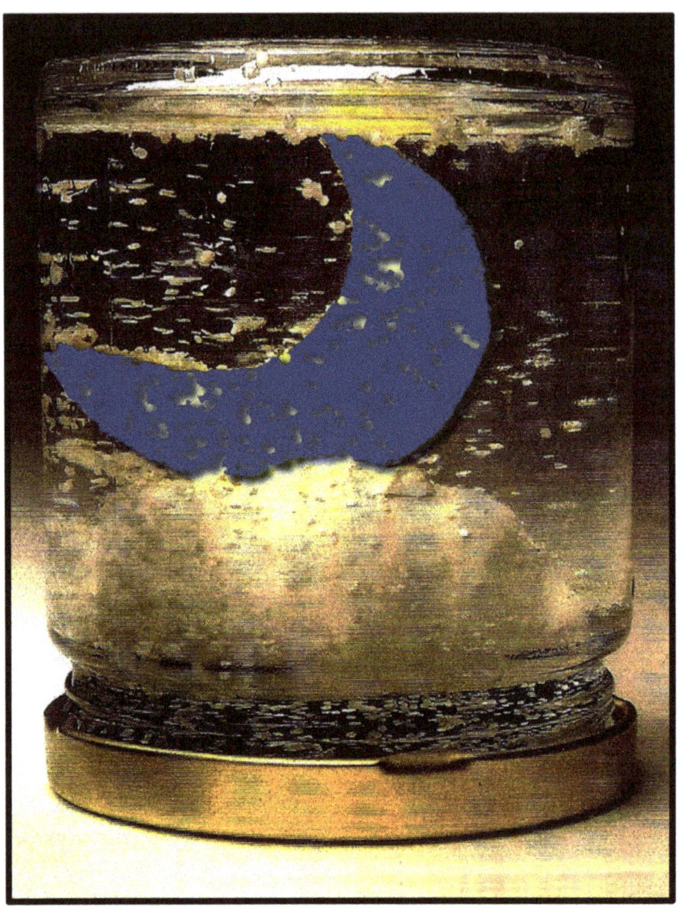

### You will need:

1 Glass jar with lid

2 Foil

3 Blue clay

4 White clay

-Or any Islamic figurine (waterproof) instead of the foil and clay

5 Plumber's Goop (waterproof glue)

6 Glitter

7 Oven

### About:

Create your own snow globe with a few simple materials. The best part is you get to choose what you want to put inside. Keep it to decorate your room or give it to friends and family as a gift.

### What to do:

1 Make a ball with the foil, cover it with white clay, and then glue it to the inside of the lid while it's upside down. Glue it in the center making sure there's still enough room to screw on the lid.

2 Create a moon from yellow clay, bake it, and then glue it to the cloud making sure it is small enough to fit inside the jar.

3 Or use any Islamic waterproof figurine that will fit in the jar.

4 Fill the jar with glitter and water then carefully place the lid and upside down figurine into the jar and screw it on tightly.

5 Flip it over to create the snow globe.

# Islamic Window Stickers

# 24

## About:

Create your very own window stickers. You pick the design and you pick where to stick them! They're great for Ramadan and Eid to decorate your house with.

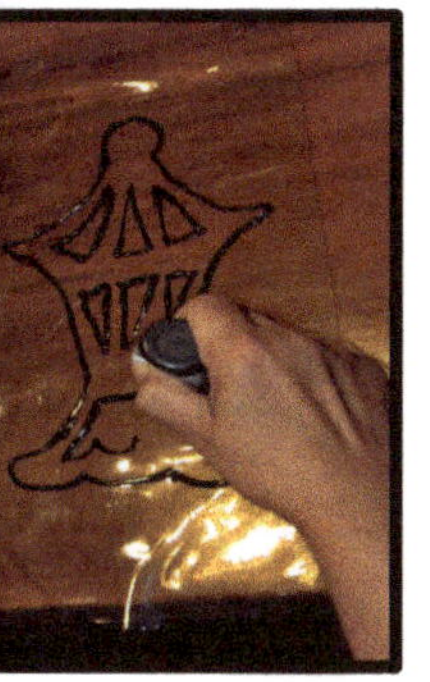

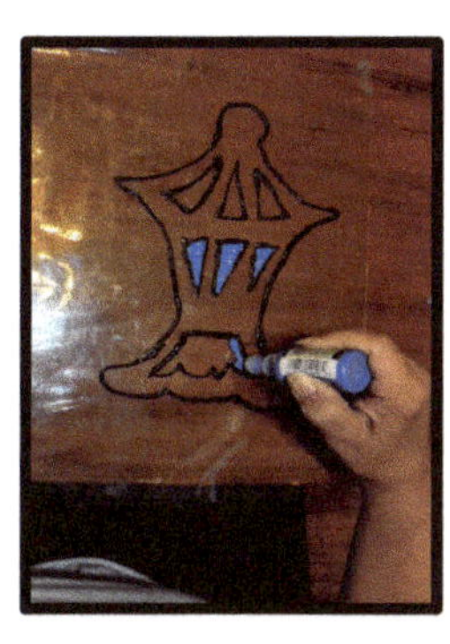

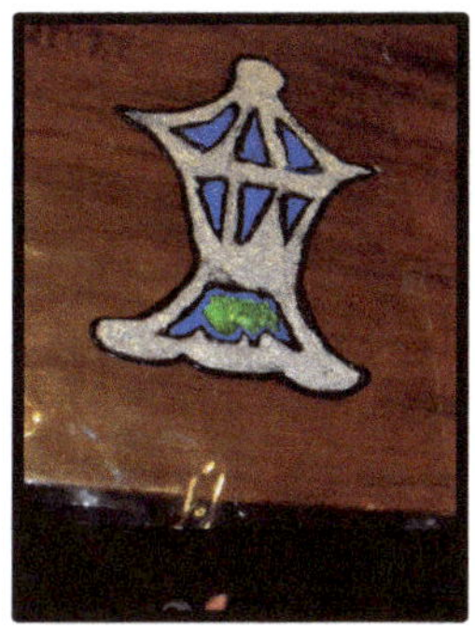

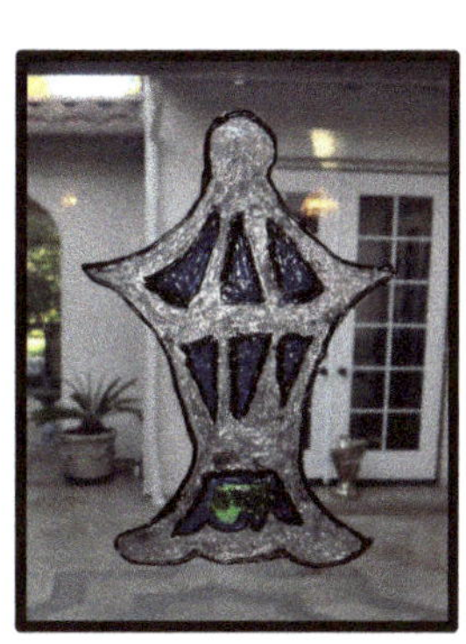

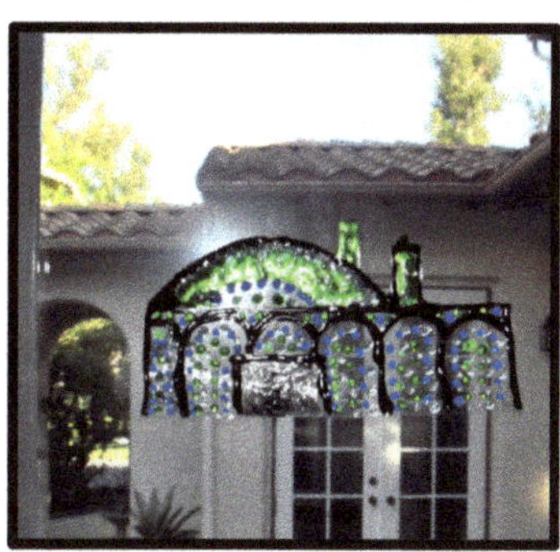

## You will need:

1 Thin plastic mat

2 3D fabric paint bottles

3 Printed design to trace

4 Scissors

5 Marker

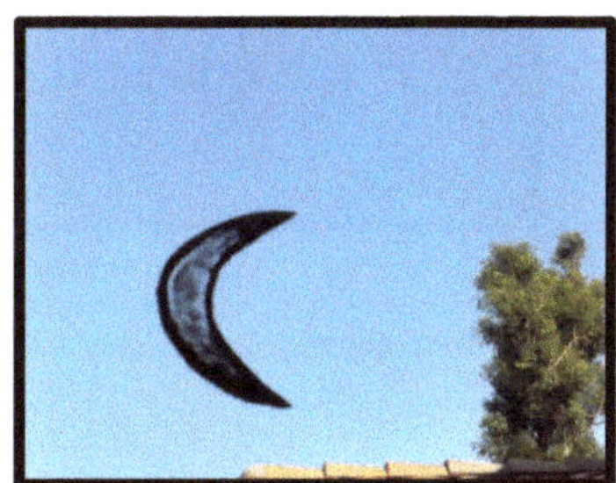

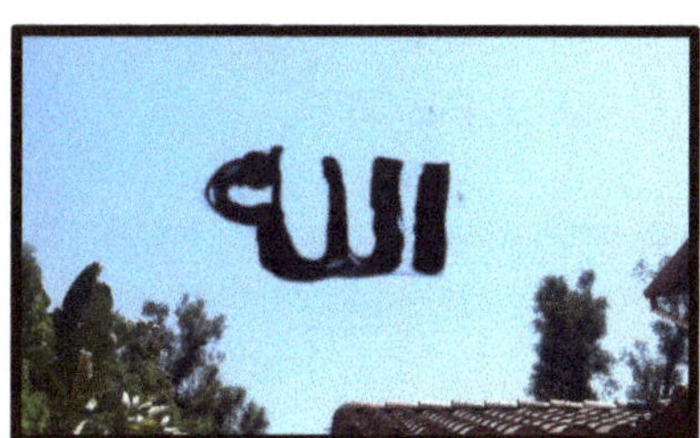


## What to do:

1 Place the printed design under the plastic mat and trace with a marker.

2 Outline the marked design with a generous layer of paint.

3 Fill in with more paint, using colors as desired.

4 Let dry, then cut around the edges.

5 The final product will stick to any glass window.

6 Make your own design for any occasion. Stickers can be peeled off and reused over and over.

# Lanterns
## 25

**About:**

Lanterns are a Ramadan staple. Create your own to hang for decoration during this blessed month.

**You will need:**

1 Four pieces of colored construction paper

2 Yarn

3 Scissors

4 Markers

5 Paint and paintbrush

6 Tape

7 Hole puncher

8 Glitter

9 Tissue paper

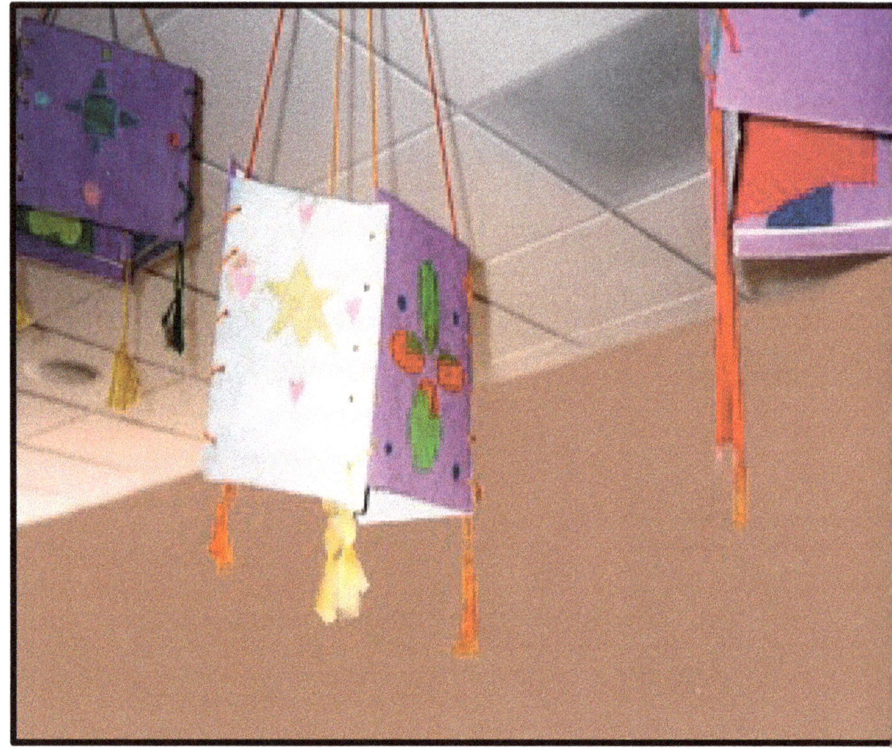

**What to do:**

1 Punch five holes along both sides of each piece of paper.

2 Decorate one side of each paper with any designs you like using paint, tissue paper, markers, glitter, etc.

3 Draw a star, or your own design, on the construction paper. Then cut it out and glue a different color of tissue paper on the back of the cut out design of the construction paper.

4 Attach each paper to the other by threading the yarn in and out of the holes.

5 Leave excess yarn at the bottom to leave hanging.

6 Tape four long pieces of yarn, one in every corner, and tie them together at the very top.

7 Hang or tape the lantern to the ceiling.

# Make Your Own Paper
## 26

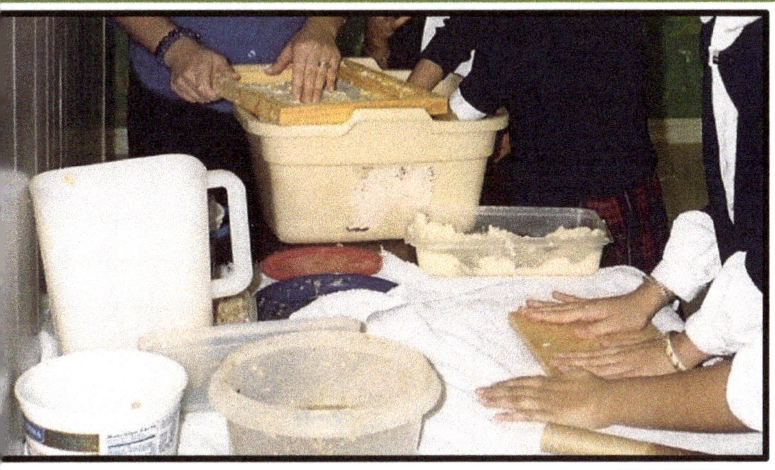

## About:

The process of creating something from scratch can be a very enlightening one. Allow your kids to experience what it's like to combine different ingredients together to make something they use almost everyday of their lives.

## You will need:

1 Bond paper

2 Paper mold

3 Blender

4 Plastic wash bin/litter box

5 Two towels

6 Two wooden boards

7 Iron

8 Glitter

9 Dried flowers

10 Starch

11 Water

12 Pot

13 Stove

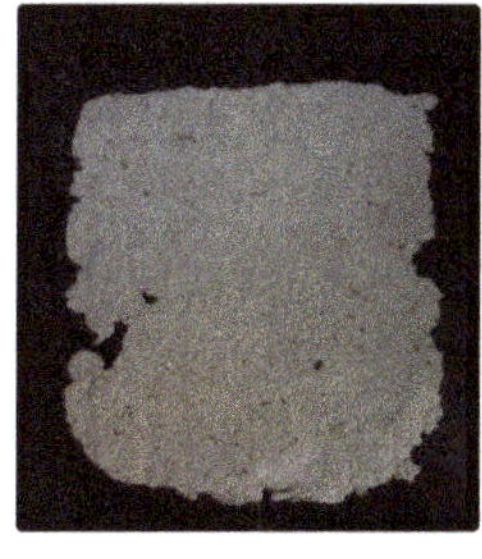

## What to do:

1 Tear the bond paper into small shreds then put them into the pot with water. Boil for 20 minutes on the stove.

2 Put mixture into blender to make pulp.

3 Fill the wash bin with water and stir in the pulp, glitter, dried flowers, and a few tablespoons of starch.

4 Dip the paper mold into the material, lift it out and let excess water drain out.

5 On the floor, lay a towel on one wooden board then lay the wet paper on the towel. Create a stack of: paper, towel, paper, towel, and the other wooden board.

6 Stand on top of the stack to press out water.

7 Separate the sheets of paper and lay them out on the towels to dry.

8 Iron the paper flat.

# Moon Rock Painting
## 27

## About:

The night before Ramadan or Eid go out with your children to site the moon. Come back and paint the moon and the stars that you saw on a rock.

## You will need:

1 3D fabric paint bottles

2 Rock

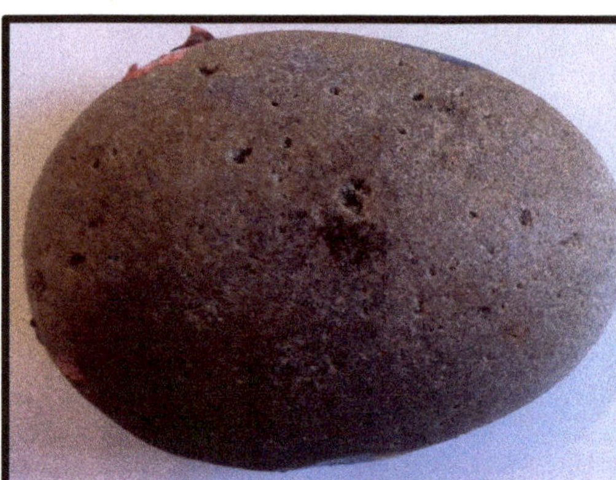

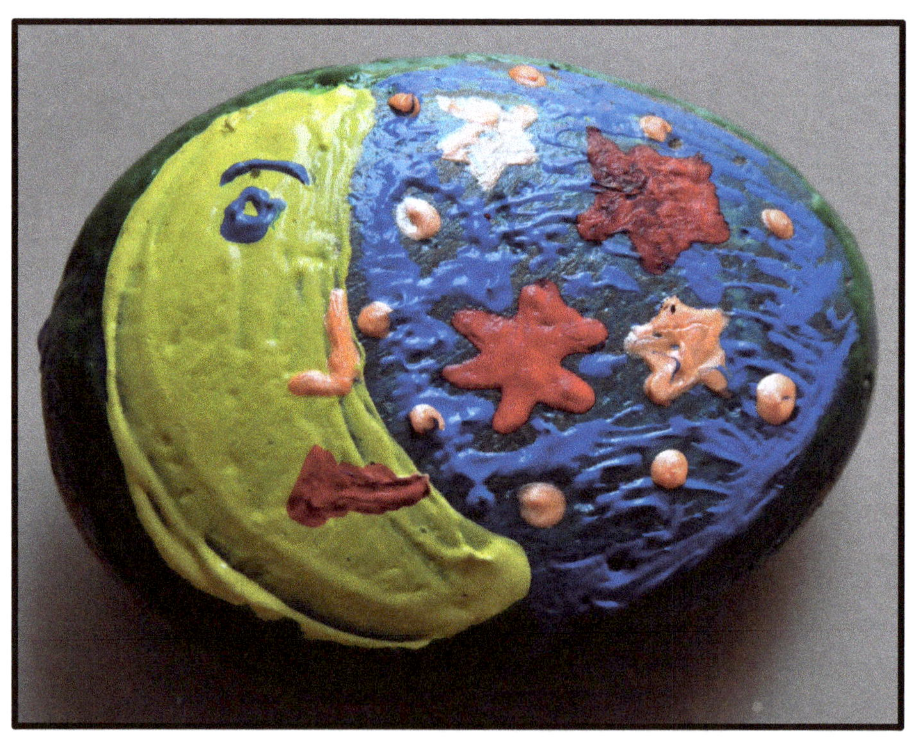

## What to do:

1 Buy a rock from a craft store or pick one up from the outdoors.

2 Using the different colors of paint make your own design of the moon and stars.

3 Leave to dry.

# Mosaic Pen Holder
## 28

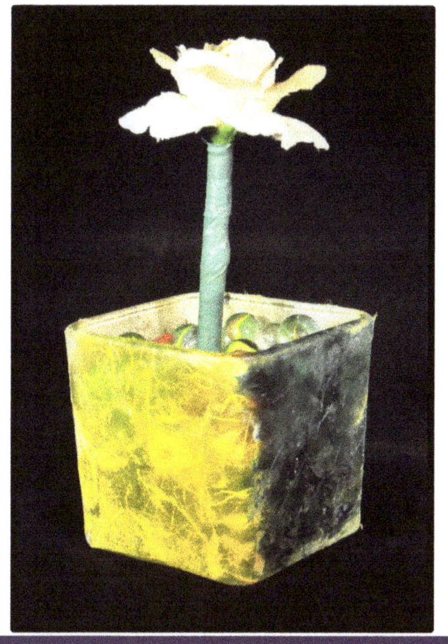

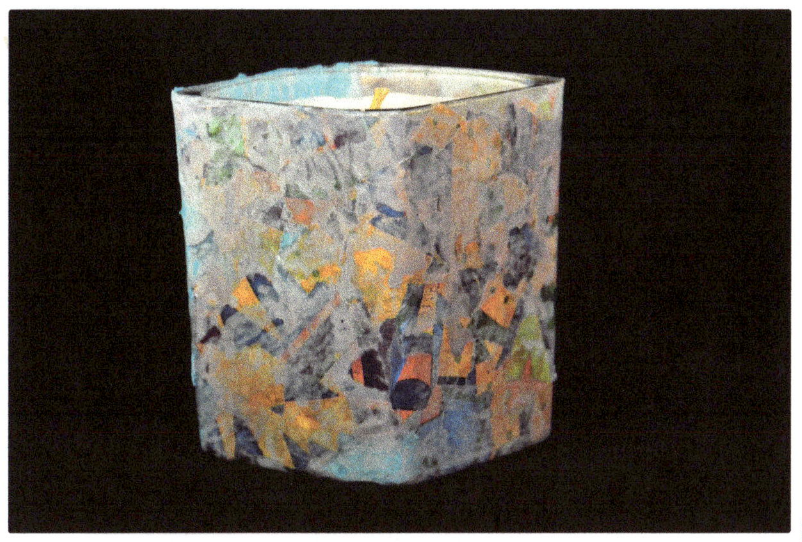

### About:

Make this beautiful Eid gift for a special person in your life.

### You will need:

1 Glass holder

2 Different colored tissue paper

3 Transparent color pickling stain - one step

4 Paintbrush

5 Pebbles or marbles

6 Green floral tape

7 Synthetic flower

8 Hot glue gun

9 Markers

10 Other decorating materials

11 Pen

### What to do:

1 Cut different colored tissue paper into small pieces.

2 Paint pickling stain on the glass holder and stick the tissue paper on it.

3 Repaint on top of the tissue paper already on the glass with another coat of pickling stain and let dry.

4 Place pebbles or marbles in the glass holder.

5 Glue the flower to the bottom of the pen.

6 Wrap the pen with green floral tape from the bottom of the pen where the flower is to the top of the pen where the point of the pen is.

7 Place pen in the holder.

# Needlepoint for Eid
29

## About:

Knit something special for Eid or Ramadan to hang in your house for decoration using Arabic writing.

## What to do:

1 Start with following the stitches for the writing and then work on the background following the number of stitches shown on the picture.

2 Use a continental stitch for the canvas.

3 Start the stitch by leaving about a one-inch tail of yarn on the backside of the canvas and bring your needle up through the hole.

4 Go back down to the backside of the canvas to the hole across, and then come up to the next square under.

5 All stitches are done in a left to right manner over and over again; make sure all stitches are going in the same direction.

6 When finished with the yarn turn the backside of the plastic canvas over and run the needle under the last four stitches then cut the yarn with scissors next to the last stitch.

7 Start over when needed till you finish your canvas.

## You will need:

1 Two colors of embroidery yarn

2 Size 20 knitting needles

3 Scissors

4 Plastic canvas

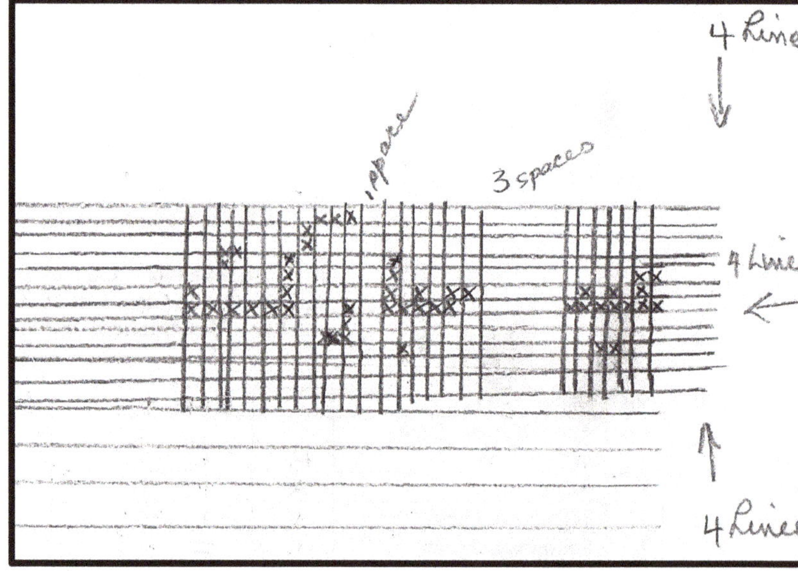


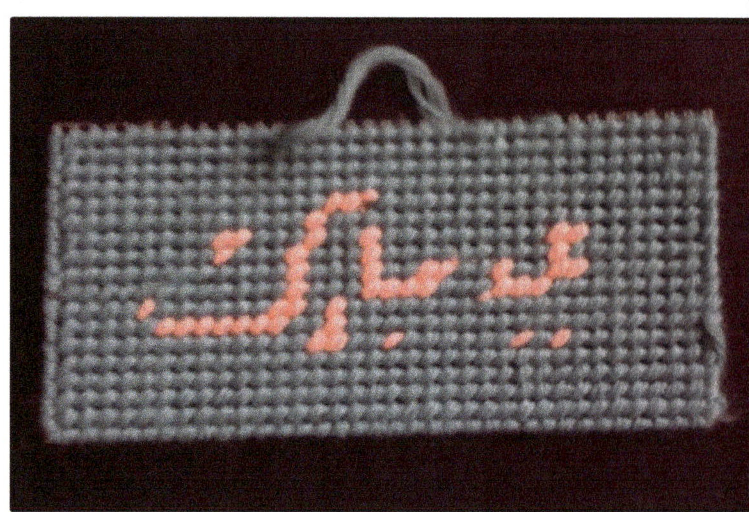

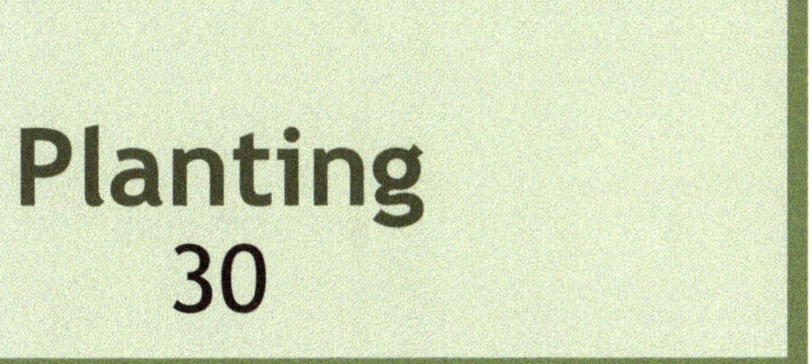


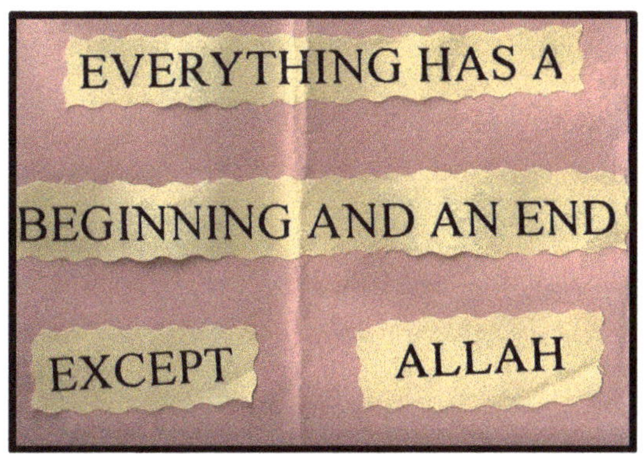


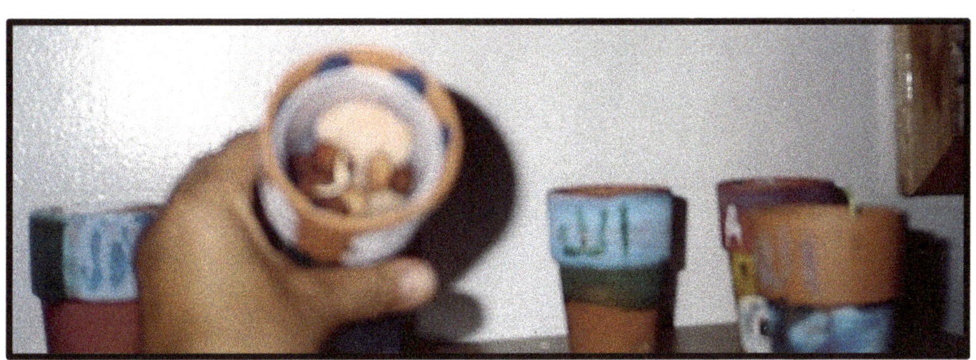

**You will need:**

1 Clay pot

2 Cotton

3 Water

4 Five fava beans

5 Plastic cup

6 Paint

7 Paintbrush

**About:**

Everything has a beginning and an end. Especially living organisms like plants. Use this project to see the process of how a plant grows then either keep it for yourself or give it as gift with a colorful pot.

**What to do:**

1 Paint the outside of the clay pot with any design you want and let it dry.

2 Put the plastic cup inside the pot.

3 Put wet cotton inside the cup.

4 Put five fava beans on the wet cotton.

5 Water the beans with a few drops of water each day.

6 Watch the beans grow.

# Prayer Tree

## 31

**About:**

Use this resourceful way to chart all the prayers. This color-coded activity will help your kids learn and memorize the different prayers, the obligatory ones (Fard), the extra (Sunnah) ones, and the Ramadan nightly prayer (Taraweeh).

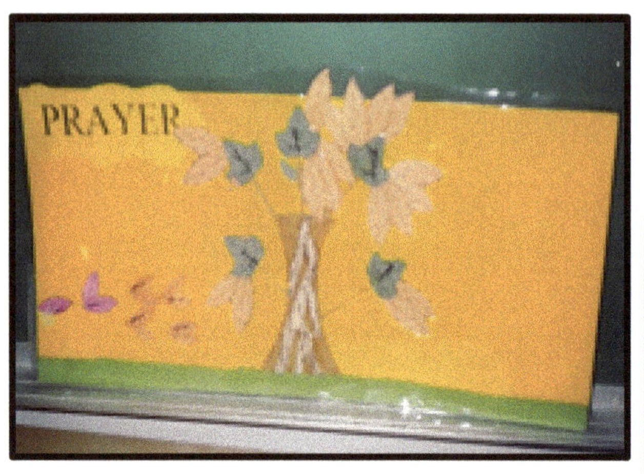


**You will need:**

1 Big yellow poster board

2 Brown construction paper

3 Green construction paper

4 Pink construction paper

5 Gray construction paper

6 Red construction paper

7 Dark green construction paper

8 Scissors

9 Pen

10 Glue

**What to do:**

1 Cut the dark green paper as grass and glue it on the bottom of the poster.

2 Use the brown paper to cut out the trunk of the tree and glue it in the middle of the poster and draw five branches.

3 Use the green paper to cut out five large leaves for the five daily Fard prayers.

4 On each leaf write the name of the prayer in Arabic or English: From right to left: Fajr, Duhr, Asr, Maghrib, Eisha, then glue them to each branch.

5 Use the pink paper to cut out 18 smaller leaves for the Sunnah prayers.

6 For each Fard prayer, attach the pink leaves as Sunnah prayers. Fagr: 2 before, Duhr: 4 before, 4 after, Asr: 4 before, Maghrib: 2 after, Eisha: 2 after.

7 Use the gray paper to cut out eight very small leaves for the Taraweeh prayer and glue them on the poster anywhere you like.

8 Use the red paper to cut three more very small leaves for the Shafaa and Witr prayer performed after the last prayer of the day and glue them on the poster anywhere you like.

# Quran Book Cover
# 32

## About:

Do you have an important book you want to cover, the Quran maybe? Design and build your own book cover to protect what's inside, making it beautiful and decorative.

## You will need:

1 Colored paper

2 Felt-tip pens

3 Scissors

4 Large, thin piece of cardboard

5 Ribbon

6 Glue

7 Tape

8 Ruler

9 Book to cover

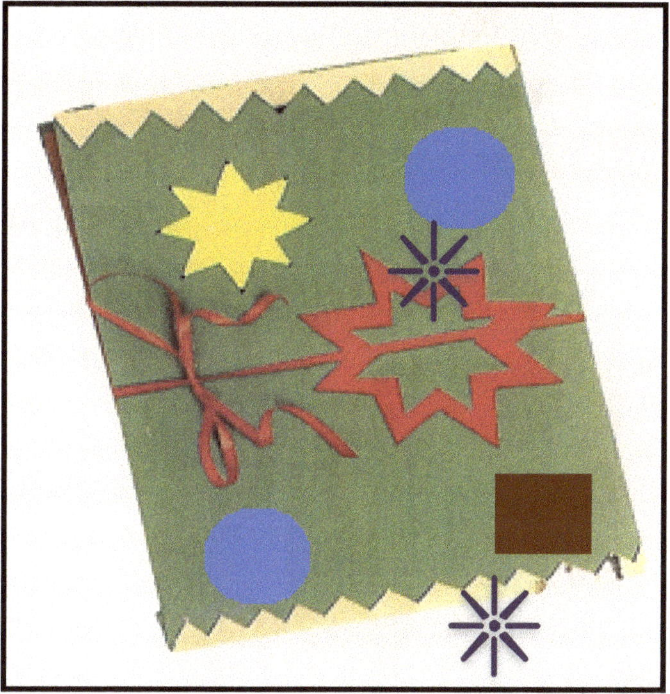

## What to do:

1 Lay your book open on the cardboard and draw around it leaving an extra ½ inch to the left and right sides on the book.

2 Cut along the lines.

3 Put the cardboard that you cut out on top of the colored paper and cut jagged edges from the paper about ½ inch thick.

4 Glue the colored paper onto the cardboard.

5 Cut out shapes using another colored piece of paper and glue them onto the cover. Or decorate the cover with the pens.

6 Attach your cover to the book by folding the edges over and tying it with ribbon.

# Ramadan Ceramic Moon

# 33

## About:

Get innovative with these ceramic moons and hang them around the house as Ramadan decorations.

## You will need:

1 Faster Plaster

2 Water

3 Moon mold

4 Toothpick

5 Paint and paintbrush

6 Microwave

7 Paper towel

8 String

9 Bowl

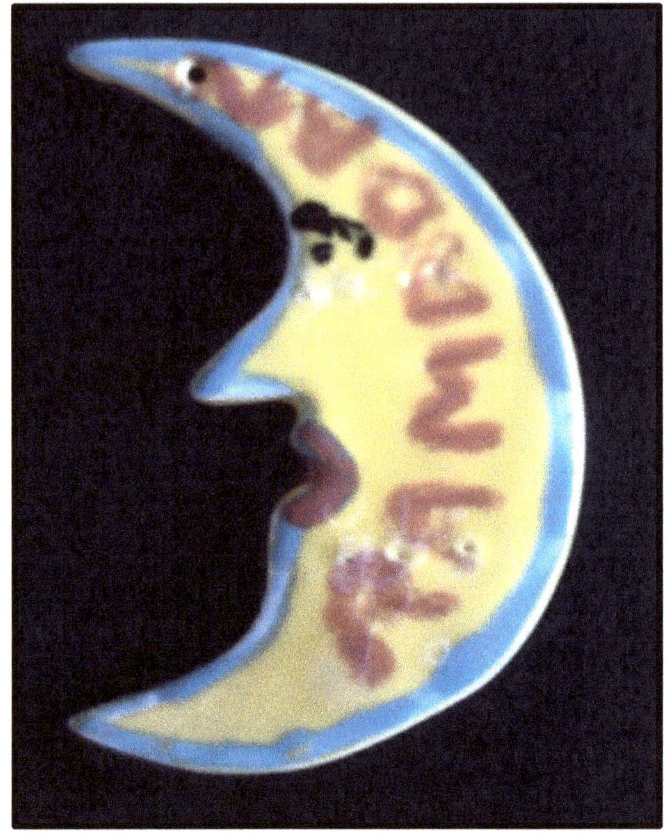

## What to do:

1 Use a ratio of two parts plaster and one part water, mix together in a bowl.

2 Pour into moon mold, lightly tapping on the edge to bring air bubbles to the surface.

3 Let plaster dry in mold for about one hour. It should feel dry to the touch but still a little damp.

4 Before it completely dries, poke a hole with a toothpick where you want to hang the moon.

5 Put the plaster on a paper towel and place in the microwave on low for about four minutes.

6 Let it cool for one minute.

7 Paint the moon and attach the string.

# Ramadan Display
## 34

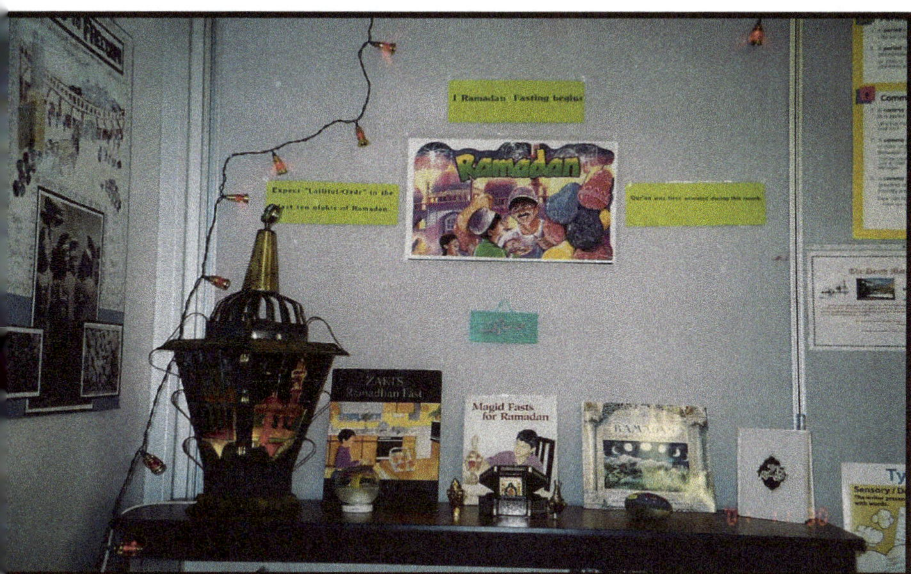


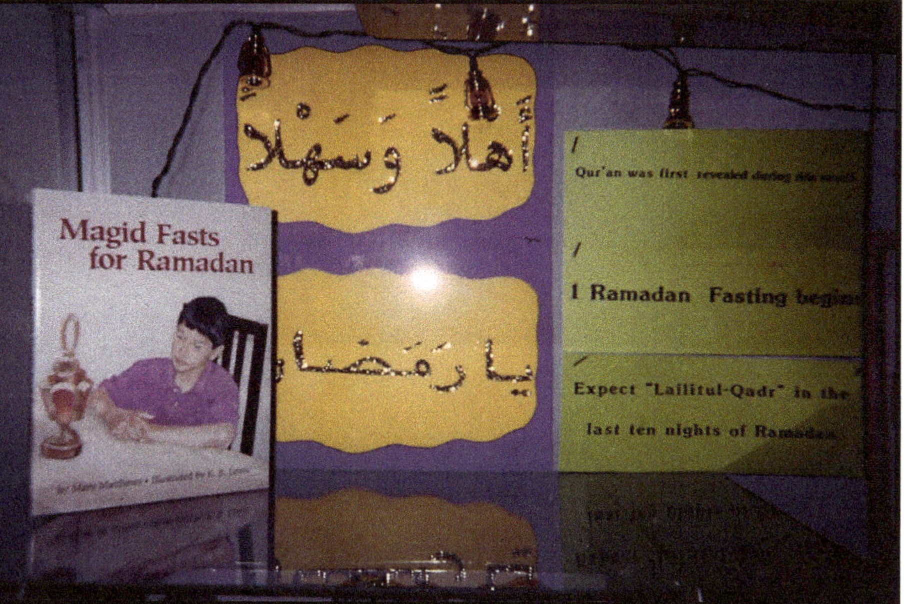


### About:

Fasting in Ramadan is another important pillar of Islam. Encourage your children to do their own 3D display about it to present in their classrooms, local library, or to their friends and family to teach others

### You will need:

1 Suggested materials:

- Lanterns
- Quran
- Poster board
- Markers, pens, crayons
- Glitter pen
- Books about Ramadan
- Lights
- Construction paper

2 Glue

### What to do:

1 Start with a poster board and write informational sentences about Ramadan.

2 Decorate the poster board.

3 On a flat surface, place a lantern, a Quran, and any other materials related to Ramadan to display.

# Ramadan Treat Platters
## 35

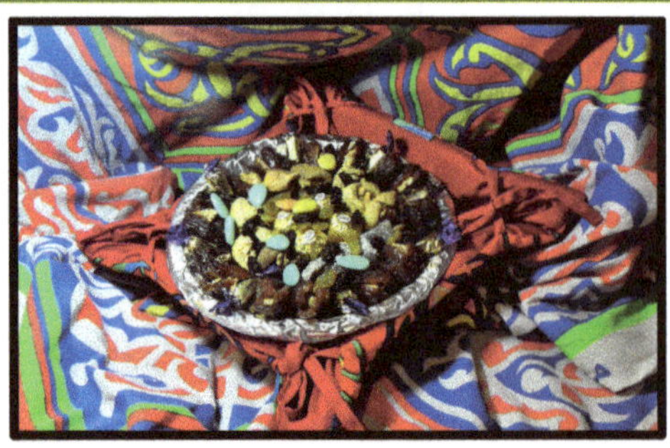

## About:

Before Ramadan, get your family together to make these delicious Ramadan Treat Platters. Fill them with all the Ramadan dried fruits and sweets. Give them to your friends, family, or keep them in the kitchen to break your fast with. Or eat them for Suhour.

## You will need:

1 Platter

2 Suggested materials:

- -Dates
- -Sugarcoated almonds
- -Dry figs
- -Dried apricots
- -Wrapped chocolates
- -Nuts
- -Raisins

3 Clear wrapping paper

4 Ramadan Kareem sticker

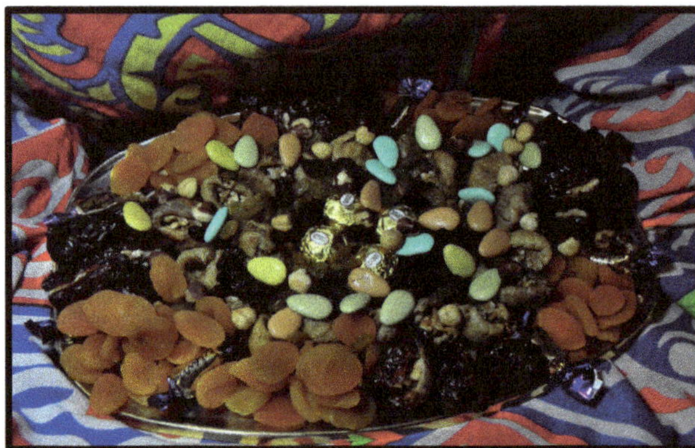

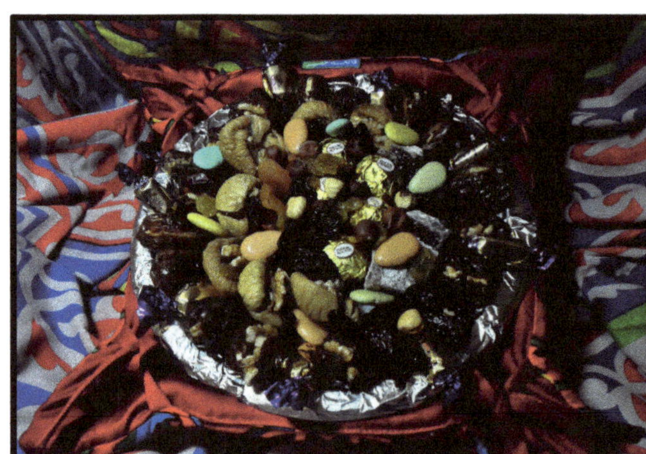

## What to do:

1 Prepare platter.

2 Arrange the treats in a decorative way.

3 Wrap the platter in clear wrapping paper and put a sticker that says, “Ramadan Kareem.”

# Sand Candles
## 36

### You will need:

1 Plastic bucket

2 Sand to fill bucket

3 Spray bottle with water

4 Liquid wax/beeswax

- One pound will make four small candles

5 Candle wick

6 Shaper/mold

7 Paint and paintbrush

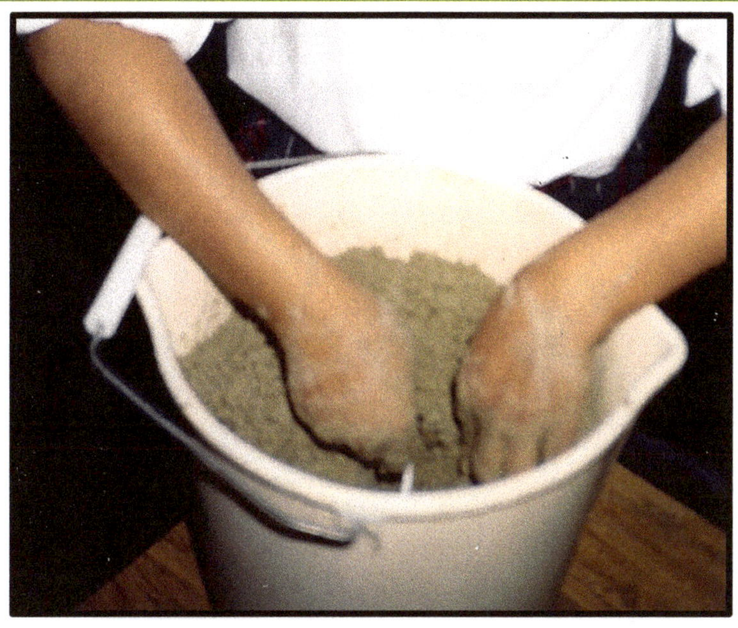

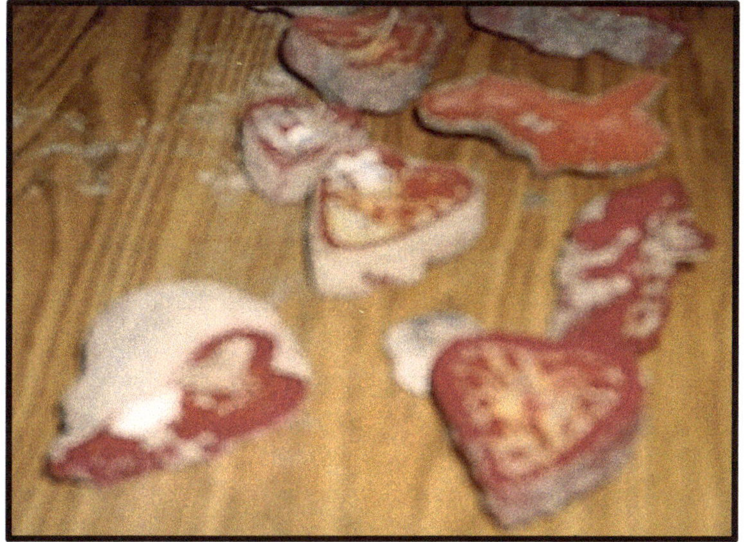

### About:

Try this very unique way of making candles. Using sand, one of Allah's basic creations.

### What to do:

1 Fill bucket with sand and dampen by spraying some water on it.

2 Put the shaper in the middle of the sand and take out any sand in the middle of the shape.

3 Make sure there is still a lot of sand at the bottom of the bucket.

4 Pour the liquid wax in the middle of the sand where you put the shaper.

5 Place the wick in the middle of the wax before it dries.

6 Let wax dry.

7 Decorate with paint.

# Shoebox Mosque

## 37

**About:**

Transform a shoebox into a beautiful mosque using simple steps.

**What to do:**

1 Paint the shoebox, inside and out, with a brick or stone color and let it dry.

2 Cut the lid of the shoebox into two pieces, the right side shorter than the left and use the shorter piece as the roof.

3 Paint that piece the same color as the rest of the shoebox, but paint one flap a different color and decorate with stickers.

4 Paint the straws, let dry, then cut them and use them as supporting columns by taping them to the flap.

5 Place the roof into the box, covering only a portion of the opening of the box. You may need to use glue on the sides so that it stays in place.

6 To make a dome, cover the top of the orange squeezer with modeling clay and let it dry. Paint the dome a different color than the box then glue it on the center of the roof.

7 Take the paper towel tube and paint it a different color.

8 Cut the bottom part of the paper cup and paint it the same color as the tube then glue it half way down the tube to make the balcony.

9 Glue the tube, now a minaret, in the bottom right corner of the box.

10 Make a small dome for the minaret by covering only the top part of the squeezer with clay, leave it to dry, and then paint it. Place it on top of the tube. Then decorate the mosque, draw a door, etc.

**You will need:**

1 Shoebox

2 Paper towel tube

3 Glue

4 Tape

5 Small paper cup

6 Four straws

7 Scissors

8 Modeling clay

9 Paint and paintbrush

10 Orange squeezer

11 Stickers

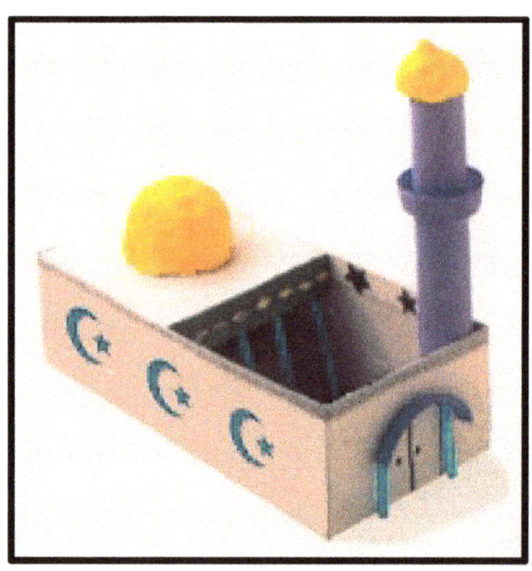

# Thankful Daisy

## 38

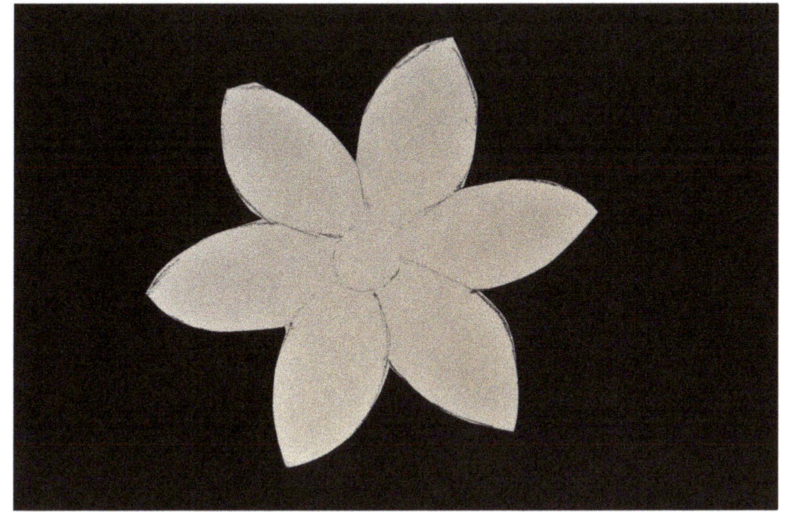

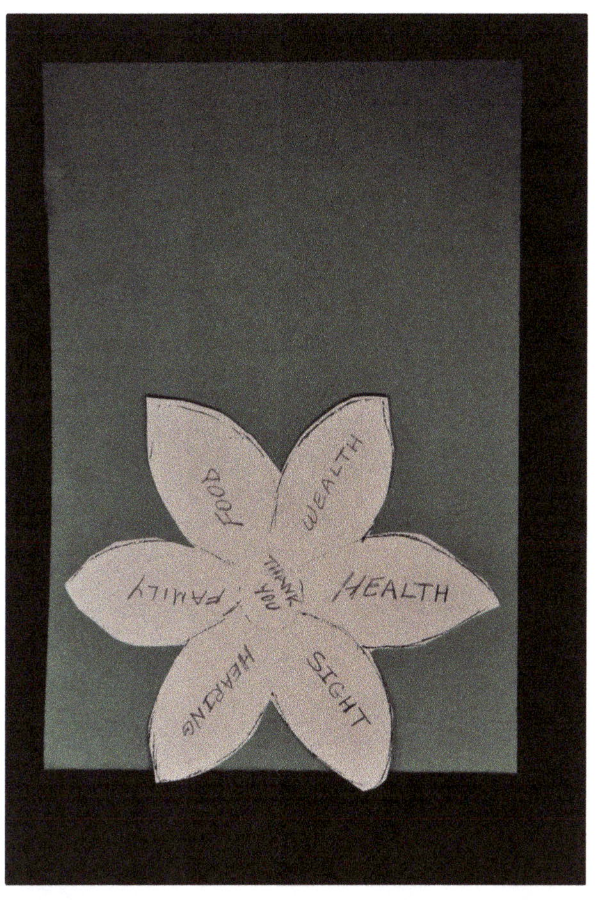


### About:

These daisies are easy to make but very important to have. Hang them on your wall to remind yourself to always thank Allah or to write things you want to improve in your life.

### You will need:

1 White paper

2 Different colored construction paper

3 Markers

4 Glue

5 Scissors

### What to do:

1 Draw a daisy on the white paper with 6 petals.

2 In the center of the daisy write “thank you.”

3 On each petal of the daisy write what you are thankful for.

4 Color the daisy and cut it out.

5 Glue it on the construction paper.

# Windmill
## 39

## About:

Make these fun windmills to play with on Eid day with your friends. If you're celebrating outdoors, take these with you and watch how one of Allah's basic creations, the wind, makes them turn in circles.

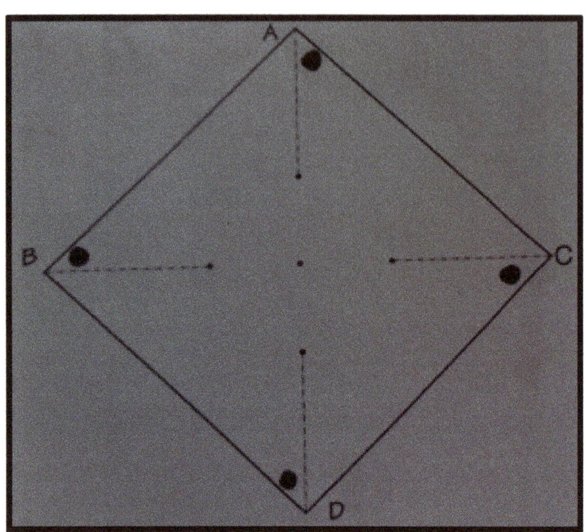


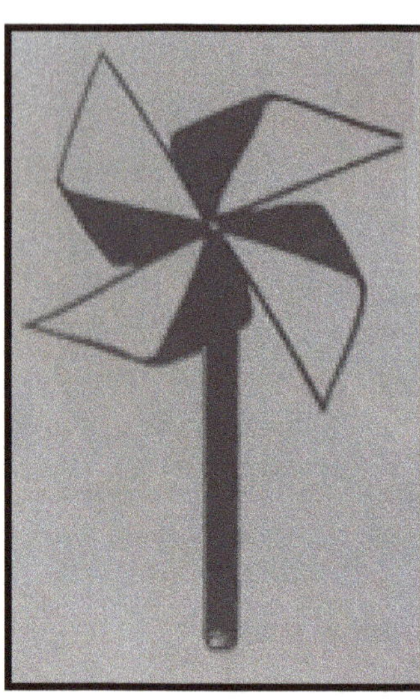

## You will need:

1 Square piece of paper

2 Marker

3 Ruler

4 Scissors

5 Plastic balloon stick

6 Pin

7 Crayons

## What to do:

1 On the square piece of paper label each corner with a letter (A,B,C,D) and rotate it into a diamond.

2 Draw a dot in the center of the diamond.

3 Draw a straight dotted line going from each corner to two inches towards the center.

4 Then cut along the dotted lines.

5 Fold the right flap of each letter into the center dot.

6 Place the pin through the center, making sure you attach each flap.

7 Attach the wheel to the plastic balloon stick with the other end of the pin, then fold the pin over for safety.

8 Color the windmill.

# Wire Ramadan Lantern

## 40

### About:

These lanterns make great Ramadan decorations. Hang them on your walls, doors, or anywhere you like.

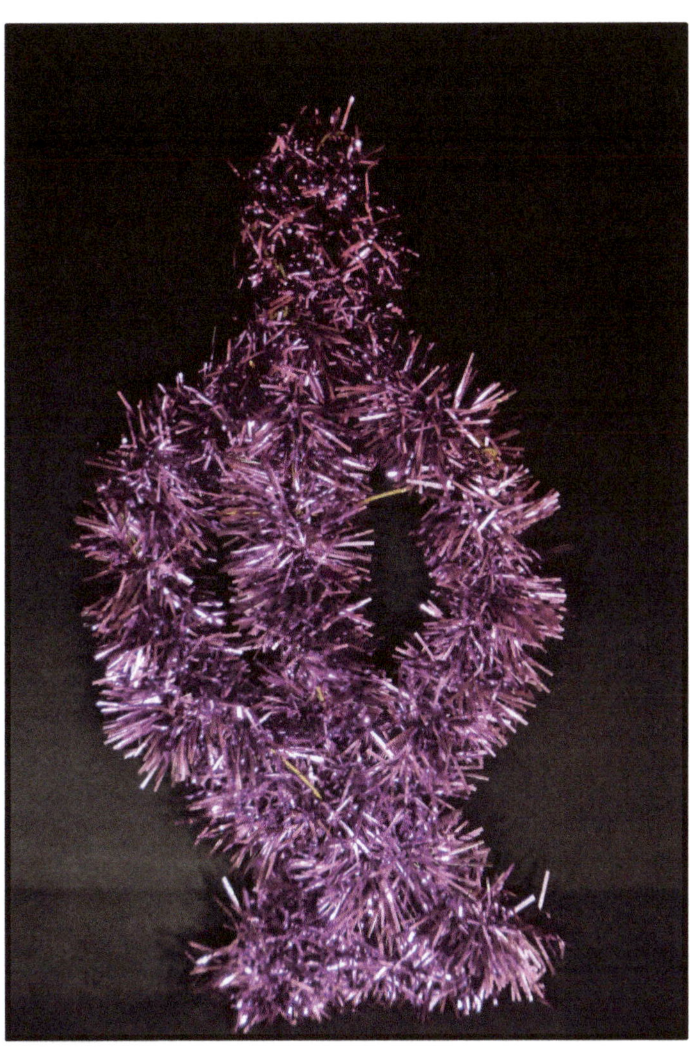

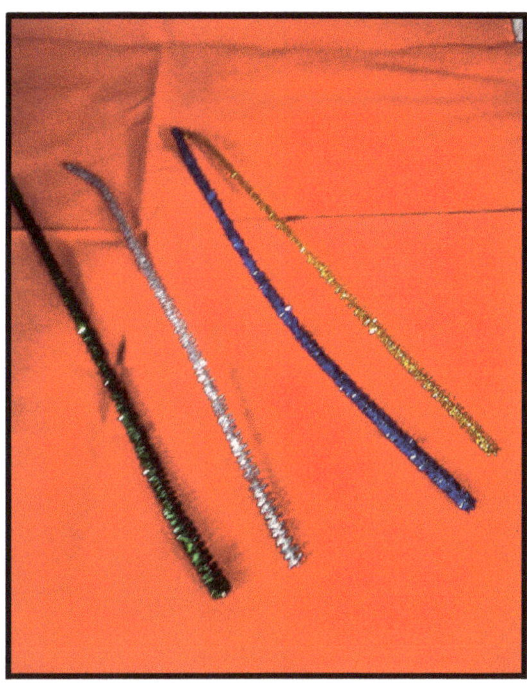

### You will need:

1 Thin wire

2 Metallic decorations

3 Scissors

### What to do:

1 Twist the thin wire into the shape of a lantern.

2 Roll the metallic decorations around the thin wire.

www.ingramcontent.com/pod-product-compliance
Lightning Source LLC
LaVergne TN
LVHW060643110826
845147LV00018B/1030

*9780615498706*